EXECUTIVE EDITOR
Natalie Earnheart

CREATIVE TEAM
Jenny Doan, Natalie Earnheart, Christine Ricks,
Tyler MacBeth, Mike Brunner, Lauren Dorton,
Jennifer Dowling, Dustin Weant, Jessica Toye,
Kimberly Forman, Denise Lane, Grant Flook

EDITORS & COPYWRITERS
Nichole Spravzoff, Camille Maddox,
David Litherland, Julie Barber-Arutyunyan,
Hillary Doan Sperry, Lora Kroush

SEWIST TEAM
Jenny Doan, Natalie Earnheart, Courtenay Hughes,
Carol Henderson, Cassandra Ratliff,
Janice Richardson

PRINTING COORDINATOR
Rob Stoebener

PRINTING SERVICES
Walsworth Print Group
803 South Missouri
Marceline, MO 64658

LOCATIONS
Fran Esry, Hamilton, MO

CONTACT US
Missouri Star Quilt Company
114 N Davis
Hamilton, MO 64644
888-571-1122
info@missouriquiltco.com

BLOCK Idea Book™ Volume 8 Issue 6 ©2021.
All Rights Reserved by Missouri Star Quilt
Company. Reproduction in whole or in part in
any language without written permission from
Missouri Star Quilt Company or BLOCK Idea Book
is prohibited. No one may copy, reprint,
or distribute any of the patterns or materials
in this magazine for commercial use without
written permission of Missouri Star Quilt Company.
Anything you make using our patterns or ideas,
it's yours!

6
SAY ALOHA TO HAWAIIAN QUILTING

Rediscover this breathtakingly beautiful quilting style and learn a few tips and techniques from renown Hawaiian appliqué expert Nancy Lee Chong.

16
THE CHONG WAY TO APPLIQUÉ

Read all about what inspired Nancy Lee Chong to start Hawaiian quilting. It may light a creative spark within you!

24
SKYWARD

Are you on the lookout for fresh inspiration? All you have to do is look up! Created with easy paper piecing, these pretty little wings truly elevate the design.

30
CANDY LANE

We couldn't help but be reminded of a favorite classic childrens' game when we created this playful paper pieced quilt. It's pure eye candy!

36
FLOWER CHAIN

Create a quaint quilted garden filled with blooming pinwheel flowers featuring petite eight pointed petals, accented with lovely Irish Chain blocks.

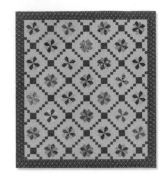

44
GET TO KNOW CHRISTOPHER THOMPSON

Style is in Christopher's DNA. With his passion for design and savvy for sewing, he became a positive influence in the quilting world.

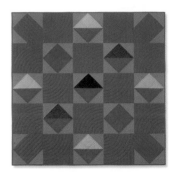

50
FOUR-PATCH TUMBLER

If you're tired of simple squares, try tumblers! These blocks have a charming vintage vibe and they stitch up in a snap.

56
MISTAKES ARE PROOF YOU'RE TRYING

Instead of fighting with your seam ripper, learn how to use it as an important tool to help your quilting and sewing projects come to life.

60

PATCHWORK TUMBLER

Forget rough and tumble, this pretty quilt couldn't be easier! And when you're through piecing, all the edges end up nice and straight without extra trimming.

66

STAR SASHED NINE-PATCH

What do you get when you put together nine-patch squares with pretty stars? You're about to find out! The addition of stars at each intersection really makes this quilt shine.

72

TUMBLER DASH

Don't walk, dash to your sewing machine to stitch up this lively version of a traditional tumbler quilt. All you have to do is add a daring little diagonal stripe.

78

TALAVERA TILE SEW-ALONG

Finish up your gorgeous Talavera Tile quilt with easy sashing to make your blocks pop! Then add the borders and you're all through. You did it!

82

BOUND IN SECRETS

The final chapter of this exciting mystery story is going to make you gasp! Don't worry, Jenny will make everything right in the end with a quick snip of her scissors.

86

JENNY'S JOURNAL

What's Jenny been up to lately? Well, you're going to adore these two festive quilts, one adorned with embroidered quilt blocks and the other with cute gnomes!

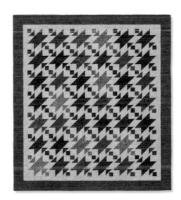

88

WANDERLUST

If traveling the world is your passion, you just might have a case of wanderlust. Take this stylish paper pieced quilt along with you and you'll be cozy wherever you roam.

96

PENGUIN MARCH GARLAND

Cute little penguins are here to brighten up your home this winter! You'll love their charming button eyes. And they're so easy to make with our Magic Circle template.

3

A note from Jenny

Dear Quilters,

As we approach the end of the year, my thoughts naturally tend to shift towards giving. It's nearly the holidays and I can't wait to share the gifts I've created and thoughtfully chosen throughout the year with my friends and family. But more than that, I have come to realize that giving is the secret to living an abundant life. Whenever I go through challenging times, if I choose to give whatever I can of my time and talents instead of keeping to myself, I feel less alone and soon the small acts of service I've performed come back to me tenfold. It has been proven to me over and over in my life.

A mindset of abundance can be cultivated no matter what our situation may be. Whether we live in wealthy or modest circumstances, there is always something we can give. Recently, I released a book about my life. It was a humbling experience to share so much with so many, but I am grateful that I did. Since that time, many people have reached out to me and I feel more connected with quilters around the world than ever before. It is a welcome feeling after so many months of isolation. It takes vulnerability to share ourselves.

Most importantly, this holiday season I want you to know how valued you are. Each week I share my creativity with you and what I receive in return is more than tenfold. Your goodness, generosity, humor, and individuality fills me up to the point of bursting! I encourage you to continue bravely showing kindness, giving freely, and sharing your beautiful creations. Thank you for showing up exactly as you are. I wish you a very Merry Christmas and a Happy New Year!

Jenny

JENNY DOAN
MISSOURI STAR QUILT CO.

GET YOUR
DIGITAL ISSUE TODAY!

Did you know that with every issue of
BLOCK Subscription you also get a
free digital copy online with exclusive
bonus content? Access it in your
Missouri Star account **RIGHT NOW!**

Hawaiian Quilting
Stitched with the Spirit of Aloha

Made in colors reminiscent of the islands' vibrant tropical landscapes featuring organic motifs that celebrate local wildlife, Hawaiian quilts are in a class all their own. These unique, two-color designs are created with needle-turn appliqué and filled with the spirit of Aloha. When you see a Hawaiian quilt for the first time, you don't forget it. It stays with you and you wonder how is it done? How do these artisans have the patience to appliqué such an expansive, intricate pattern onto the top of a quilt? How are all those tiny curves so perfectly finished? Who imagined these fabulous designs? Could I ever make a Hawaiian quilt myself? Of course you can! There is time and patience involved, but we also have a few tips and techniques from renown Hawaiian appliqué expert Nancy Lee Chong to help your journey go smoothly.

When creating a Hawaiian quilt, it's important to understand the spirit behind these stunning quilt designs. They are made with sincere intent, filled with "Aloha" or good wishes and plenty of love. In Hawaiian the word "Aloha" translates to both hello and goodbye, but it also conveys a much deeper meaning. Aloha is all about the connection between your mind and heart. And when you create Hawaiian quilts, that connection is literally made tangible in your beautiful finished design.

Lore surrounding Hawaiian quilts reminds us that when you make a quilt, it is filled with your "mana" or the strength of your spirit. So, in turn, you must treat what you create with great respect. Don't sit on your quilt, but be sure to sleep beneath it once before you give it away to restore your mana so you have the energy to continue being creative. Take the time to give thanks for your creation and for the joy it has brought you to bring it into the world. There are also some harmless superstitions surrounding Hawaiian quilting: do not use black fabric in quilts as it is considered an unlucky color, avoid depicting people or animals in quilts, don't show your quilt until it is finished, and don't steal anyone else's design. But do feel free to ask for permission as many Hawaiian quilt designs are traditional and are shared from quilter to quilter.

There is no exact history of how Hawaiian quilts came to be, but most likely the art of sewing and quilting was taught as foreigners and missionaries came to Hawaii after it was discovered by Captain James Cook in 1778. Prior to this time, many different groups of Pacific Islanders made a handcrafted type of fabric called "tapa" that was created from the bark of the "wauke" or mulberry tree. It is still created to this very day. This long process takes weeks to accomplish. The inner bark is stripped off, soaked overnight, and then pounded thin with a special wooden mallet. Thin strips become wider and wider as they are pounded. After the tapa is pounded and dried, many strips are joined together to make a larger piece of cloth. It is often dyed with natural plant dyes and carved, stamped, or painted with intricate patterns.

When traders came to the islands, they brought with them materials like fabric, needles, and thread that allowed Hawaiians to take their skills and apply them in new ways to create "kapa" or Hawaiian quilts. Some stories about the origin of Hawaiian quilting tell the tale of a Hawaiian woman seeing the shadow of a breadfruit tree on a white sheet that was laid out to dry on the grass, which inspired her to create a quilt with a similar design. There is even an account of an early Hawaiian sewing lesson, which took place in 1820, on a ship called the "Thaddeus." Lucy Thurston, the wife of an American missionary, recorded this event in her diary. She helped teach the Hawaiian queen, Kalakua, along with a group of other women, how to sew a western-style dress. But no matter how it came about, there's no denying that Hawaiian quilting is absolutely one-of-a-kind.

Hawaiian Island Colors & Symbols

Hawai'i
Red: Lehua, flower of the Ohi'a tree
Maui
Pink: Lokelani, rose
Moloka'i
Green: Kukui, flower of the Candlenut tree
Kaho'olawe
Gray: Hinahina, silversword plant
Lana'i
Orange: Kaunaoa, vine with orange stems
O'ahu
Yellow: Ilima, shrub with yellow flowers
Kaua'i
Purple: Mokihana, citrus tree
Ni'ihau
White: Pupu, tiny seashells

Typically created in high-contrast color palettes consisting of two or more colors, Hawaiian quilts focus on organic shapes like breadfruit, ginger, hibiscus, pineapple, and plumeria. The echo quilting radiates outward from the appliquéd shapes like waves lapping on the beach. Much different from traditional patchwork designs, these large-scale patterns fill the entire quilt top with a mirrored symmetrical design, like paper snowflakes created in school, but much more sophisticated in their attention to detail. Each island has a signature color and flower, but there are also many more color combinations and motifs that convey deeper meanings.

For example, breadfruit, which was perhaps the first Hawaiian quilting motif, is thought to bring abundance. A home with this quilt pattern in it will always have plenty. The anthurium is considered good luck and is a symbol of hospitality. Hibiscus flowers are associated with beauty. Plumeria are a symbol of new beginnings and are popular in baby quilts and wedding quilts. Kukui are a symbol of peace and wisdom. And there are many, many more.

Now it's time to dig into some tips from Nancy Lee Chong, a Hawaiian quilting expert, to help you get started with this beautiful style of quilting and learn how needle-turn appliqué is accomplished. She does say, "Hand appliqué really needs to be seen, instead of read about," but continues on with a few of her favorite suggestions to help lead you to success:

- Use a thin needle in the length you like. Nancy likes a long milliner's needle, size 10 for regular cottons and size 11 for batiks. A thicker needle is just harder to pull through for each stitch.

- Use the best quality thread you can afford— Nancy's favorite is Aurifil 50 weight thread.

- Always use a thread color that best matches the color of your appliqué fabric. If you can't find the perfect color match, then let the background fabric color lead you to the right choice.

Nancy adds, "Everyone is different, so don't be afraid to try different needles and threads until you find the ones that fit you perfectly. By the way, milliner needles are so thin they tend to bend, and that's exactly how I like them. I've bent them in my grip and then they don't spin around, and my thread doesn't get knotted so easily."

We asked Nancy a series of questions on how she likes to approach needle-turn appliqué and her answers are insightful and inspiring.

Is Hawaiian needle-turn appliqué different from the kind of needle-turn appliqué common in quilting today?

"I teach needle-turn applique very much like I was taught. Needle-turn appliqué is much much easier to do than the way I see being taught on the internet. As the name says: you use your needle to tuck under the seam allowance just ahead of where you are going to add your stitches. With just a little practice it becomes second nature to use your needle (that you are already holding) to tuck under your own personal seam allowance (mine is ³⁄₁₆")."

Try different color combinations to see what you prefer. Do you want the appliqué design to be the darker color or the background color? Each has a unique overall effect.

Do you recommend using any glue or fusible? Why or why not?

"Absolutely not! There is no need to add an unknown chemical or a stiffener to a quilt (or even a wall hanging). I am a purist! I like the feel of fabric, thread, and batting. Everything else just seems like someone who didn't learn how to make a traditional Hawaiian quilt for their first quilt. Our quilting ancestors made amazing quilts for hundreds of years with just fabric, thread, and batting. I never apply anything to my fabrics, as they may stiffen or cause discoloration in the future. I fell in love with cotton fabrics, and can't understand why anyone would need to add glue or fusible. I use (temporary) basting thread or straight pins to hold the fabric in place."

What kind of fabric do you prefer to use in your quilts?

"I use good quality 100% cotton fabric. I love batiks, but they are made with thinner threads that are more tightly woven, and so hand quilting is a bit more of a challenge. I like fabrics that read as solids or almost solids—like some batiks.

Traditional Hawaiian patterns examples

breadfruit

bird of paradise

monstera

pineapple

hibiscus

anthurium

kukui

angel's trumpet

plumeria

laua'e fern

The most important thing to remember when choosing the two fabrics for the top is contrast-contrast contrast! Using a light fabric with a medium fabric isn't going to provide a strong visual contrast when it's all cut and sewn. Think light on dark or dark on light—stay away from mediums for best visual impact."

What kind of color schemes are popular in Hawaiian quilting?
"The earliest quilts were made with solid fabrics brought to the Islands by missionaries and traders. Most of my quilts have been made from solids because the quilting stitches show up much more than on prints. Traditional Hawaiian quilt tops are made from two strongly-contrasting cotton fabrics. Any color scheme that offers a contrast between

the two fabrics will work. It's all about what the quilter wants to spend time with, and what the recipient may like. For example, I don't ask my grandchildren what their favorite colors are because by the time I get the quilt made, those favorite choices might have changed! I make the quilt in the colors that I want to work with and that I think will be loved by the recipient."

"White and light colors for the background with any other color for the appliqué is always a good choice. Be careful if you use a dark fabric for the background and a light fabric for the appliqué, as the seam allowance may show lighter where there are now two layers of the lighter appliqué fabric. This is sometimes called 'shadowing.' Black fabric on a Hawaiian quilt is considered bad luck."

Do you like to do the traditional echo quilting style for your Hawaiian quilts? Should Hawaiian quilts always be finished in this manner?
"Oh yes! I am very much a traditionalist. Should Hawaiian quilts always be finished in this manner? It is not for me to dictate to quilters how they should quilt their project, but echo quilting is such an easy way to distribute the stitches evenly across the quilt surface—and they make the appliqué design look more 'important.' It's part of what drew me to begin making Hawaiian quilts in the first place."

Now that you've gotten a glimpse into the art of Hawaiian quilting, why not give it a try with Nancy's very first quilt design, the beautiful Plumeria, in a smaller pillow-sized block. It's sure to add a touch of island style to your home.

CONNIE SAYLERS

Connie first met Nancy Lee Chong in her local quilt guild in Gold Beach, Oregon. Nancy taught Connie the art of needleturn appliqué and Connie found herself hopelessly addicted to this beautiful artform. They became great friends and Connie delved even deeper into Hawaiian quilting. When Nancy and her sister decided it was time to sell their quilting company, Pacific Rim Quilts, Connie and her husband, Mark, purchased the business and have been running it ever since. Connie said, "Quilting has become my favorite pastime and now it will become my life's vocation, following my passion."

materials

PROJECT SIZE
21" x 21"

PROJECT SUPPLIES
½ yard appliqué fabric
¾ yard background fabric
- includes pillow back

BACKING
¾ yard

BINDING
¼ yard

BATTING
22" x 22" square

> **APPLIQUÉ PATTERN**
> msqc.co/plumeriablock

1 prep

SELECT FABRIC & THREAD

Most people are happier with two fabrics that have strong contrast, and that read as solids, or near solids. Batiks and hand dyed fabrics are particularly good choices. Buy the best fabric you can afford. It takes time to make a Hawaiian quilt, and you want the quilt to last a long time. Select thread to match the appliqué fabric. From Fabric A, cut (1) 5" and (1) 4" strip across the width of the fabric.

WASH

To preshrink and remove excess dye, wash the fabric.

FOLD and PRESS

Fold and press both the appliqué and background fabrics into eighths, right sides together, pivoting around the center of the fabric, as illustrated below.

Fold and press both the appliqué fabric and the background fabric identically, but separately. Press in TEMPORARY fold guidelines using a warm (not hot), dry iron. When pressing on the bias fold (created with the 3rd fold), be sure to lift the iron and firmly place on the fold, rather than sliding the iron along the fold. Leave fabrics folded until instructed to open them in later steps.

The folds in the background fabric will be used in Steps 9-11 as registration marks to help position the appliqué fabric.

2 trace & cut

Trace the appliqué pattern onto another piece of paper to preserve the master pattern. Trace only the solid cutting lines. Transfer key words "center," "straight fold," and "bias fold" onto the traced paper pattern. Cut out the traced paper pattern.

PATTERN PLACEMENT

Place the pattern on folded appliqué fabric. It is very important to align the center, straight edge, and bias edge of the pattern with the center, straight fold and bias folds of the fabric. If you do not, the pattern very likely will not fit on your fabric.

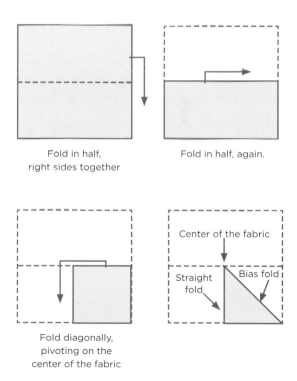

Fold in half,
right sides together

Fold in half, again.

Fold diagonally,
pivoting on the
center of the fabric

Center of the fabric

Straight fold

Bias fold

Once the pattern is in place, pin the pattern to the fabric. You only need enough pins to hold the pattern in place while you draw around it. Pinning through just one or two layers of fabric is fine at this point.

TRACE

Draw the pattern onto the appliqué fabric. Draw around the edge of the traced paper patterns. Do not add seam allowances. A ³⁄₁₆" seam allowance has already been added to the original pattern. Since you are tracing the cutting line, you can use a pencil, permanent fabric marker, or other marking tool that will show on the appliqué fabric. Do not use a ball point pen.

REMOVE PAPER

Unpin and remove the paper pattern. RE-PIN through all eight layers of fabric to hold it securely in place. Now, use lots of pins, and place pins only on the 'inside' of the design. This will help you know what to cut and what not to cut in the next step.

CUT FABRIC

Using sharp scissors, cut along lines, through all eight layers of fabric. Leave the pins in until instructed to remove them later.

UNFOLD FABRIC

Unfold the background fabric and lay it right side facing up on a table. Find the section in the background fabric that has three "down" folds together

(on the straight, the bias, and the straight). This is the section where you will begin to lay out the appliqué fabric (Section A). Place that section close to you and lightly tape the background fabric to the table to avoid shifting.

APPLIQUÉ PLACEMENT

Place the appliqué in Section A, pins facing up. Remove the pins, but leave the appliqué folded for now. Carefully align the center, straight folds, and bias folds of the appliqué fabric with the folds of the background fabric. Notice that the bias fold has more bulk than the straight folds, so position the bias fold of the appliqué slightly inside the bias fold of the background fabric. When the appliqué fabric is unfolded this bias fold will fall into the fold on the background fabric.

The appliqué fabric needs to be in its most natural, relaxed position (no ripples in the edges, nothing stretched out of shape, no overlapping pieces). The appliqué was cut out of a single, flat piece of fabric, so it must lay flat again. Before you proceed make sure the bottom layer is in its relaxed position, gently rub your fingers along any parts of the appliqué which need to be coaxed into position.

PIN THE APPLIQUÉ

Pin the bottom after the appliqué is in its proper position. Pin the bottom layer only. Only the bottom layer remains in this position, the other seven layers will open up and be placed elsewhere on the background fabric. Add pins where you can easily get them in the appliqué fabric. You will get to add more pins once the appliqué is entirely opened up.

UNFOLD THE APPLIQUÉ

Once the bottom layer is pinned, unfold the top FOUR layers of fabric. These will open along the bias fold. Position the appliqué in this section, and pin the bottom layer. Then unfold the top TWO layers of fabric. Position this quarter of the design in place, and pin the bottom layer. Unfold the top single layer, position this half of the design aligning with the folds of the background fabric, and pin.

Once the entire appliqué is fully opened and in position, add enough pins so the fabric will not shift while you thread baste it in place.

BASTE

Using a thread which contrasts in color to the appliqué fabric, thread-baste around the entire appliqué fabric. Keep basting stitches at least ½" inside the cut edge so the basting stitches will not interfere with the appliqué process. Remove the pins as you baste.

IRON

Using a hot iron (with steam if necessary), iron out all the temporary fold lines.

APPLIQUÉ

Appliqué as desired. We recommend the needleturn method, using approximately a ³⁄₁₆" turn-under seam allowance.

JOIN THE BLOCKS

Sew the blocks together (if you have more than one block) with or without sashing, as you prefer.

SANDWICH THE LAYERS

The backing fabric and batting should be a few inches larger than the quilt top. Use masking tape to secure the backing fabric (right side down) on a surface suitable for basting. Position the batting on top of the backing fabric and lightly tape it down. Center the quilt top, right side up, on the batting and lightly tape it down.

BASTE THE LAYERS TOGETHER

Using an ugly colored thread will encourage you to keep quilting just so you can pull out the ugly basting thread as you quilt. To keep the edges of your quilt from fraying as you quilt, turn the edges of the backing fabric over the batting and quilt top to enclose the edges, secure using a long whip stitch.

CHOOSE QUILTING THREAD

Old Hawaiian quilts were quilted with white thread because that was what was available. We now have colored quilting thread available, so choose the thread color(s) you prefer to enhance your quilt.

QUILT

Begin quilting in the center and work your way out to the edge of the quilt. Quilt "in the ditch" around the appliqué as you quilt from the center out.

Suggested quilt lines are shown as dashed lines on the pattern page. These are only suggestions, you may vary the quilting as you like. Echo quilting lines on a quilt this size are spaced approximately ½" apart.

FINISH

Bind, add a label, and a sleeve or make into a lovely pillow. Then enjoy your appliqué pillow with pride for many, many years.

APPLIQUÉ PATTERN
msqc.co/plumeriablock

Be sure to check out
pacificrimquilts.com

The Chong Way to Appliqué

with Nancy Lee Chong

Meet Nancy Lee Chong, the queen of Hawaiian quilting. This gentle, slow-stitching method of needle-turn appliqué takes time and patience, and watching Nancy quilt is incredibly soothing. She grew up learning how to sew from her mother, and, contrary to her calm demeanor, she describes herself as an excessively active child who didn't have much patience for detailed tasks. She said, "Because I hated to sit still, I only sewed small projects on the sewing machine because they could be completed in one or two days." She knitted pot holders and sewed quick outfits on the sewing machine, but she never imagined that she would someday develop a deep love of sewing. Later on in life, when she discovered Hawaiian quilts, everything changed.

Nancy saw her first Hawaiian quilt in 1977, at a craft fair in Honolulu, while she was living in Hawaii. The high price tag initially shocked her, but she couldn't forget about that stunning quilt. She said, "When I left I knew I had to find someone who would teach me how to make a bed-sized Hawaiian quilt." And a few months later, she was able to find a locally-famous Hawaiian quilter named Luika Kamaka who taught a weekly class at the nearby Fashion Fabrics store in Kailua. Nancy says Luika "was the perfect teacher for me, because she taught me how it was done traditionally, and insisted that I do it that way too. I chose the fabrics, created my own design, and learned how to do needle-turn applique, while working on my own creation—which was the tradition. It was such a unique experience, I still remember (43 years later) how empowering it was—and still is."

She joined the class with enthusiasm and immediately found her niche. Sitting on the floor, in view of the store's front window, Nancy and her classmates worked diligently on their Hawaiian quilts. Passers by would occasionally peek in and marvel at what they were doing. Luika assisted whenever they had questions or were ready for the next step. This simple class was a turning point for Nancy. She said, "That day changed my life in many ways, one of which was to learn that taking time to make something by hand isn't a waste of time at all."

Hawaiian quilting provided a peaceful experience for Nancy and helped her discover important attributes in herself. When she began the class she said, "I started that evening with a short list of things I needed to do before next week's session, and I've never stopped. Hawaiian quilts, and especially making Hawaiian quilts, keeps me calm." She explains further, "I discovered that I could sit still and work on something that was important and worthy of the time it took to complete. Before then, if I couldn't start and finish in 2 days, it never got done." That's the beauty of Hawaiian quilting. It causes those who engage with it to slow down and focus on the process. It very much speaks to the Hawaiian spirit of Aloha.

Hawaiian quilting designs draw from the lush flora and fauna on the islands and Nancy's first design was a plumeria flower because it had deep meaning for her, and it remains one of her favorites to this day. Traditionally, plumeria symbolize birth, love, and new beginnings. Every Hawaiian quilt has a special meaning for the maker and the recipient—these quilts are incredibly unique, made from the heart, and, Nancy said, "making them by hand gives the quilter an even deeper connection to the recipient." She loves designing quilts with Hawaiian flowers and plants, but she has also made quilts with themes from other locales and cultures including tulips, snowflakes, musical instruments, and even a Victorian gingerbread design from a house she often passed by in Snohomish, Washington, when she went to visit her sister.

Her inspiration flows from observation and all she has to do is pay attention to her surroundings. She says, "I just look around me and see (and photograph) amazing flowers and plants. When it's time to design another quilt, I choose one or two that speak to me, and figure out how to show off it's uniqueness." That's the beauty of Hawaiian quilt designs, because they are organic, they aren't constrained by what has been created before.

Designing and creating quilts has been Nancy's livelihood for years. When she relocated from Hawaii back to the Seattle area in 1980, she brought her passion for quilting with her. She taught her sister how to quilt.

She soon found herself being invited to teach at local quilt guilds and beyond. She said, "I began teaching members of the local Hawaii Club, and they suggested that we make those designs available to others in the club. My sister's business acumen and creativity gave me courage, and in 1991, we created Pacific Rim Quilt Company."

In 2015, while she was living in Gold Beach, Oregon, Nancy and her sister decided it was time to sell the company; and it turned out that her best friend, Connie, along with her husband, Mark, wanted to purchase the business. Now Connie and Mark Sayler are the wonderful owners of Pacific Rim Quilt Company and you can still find Nancy's beautiful quilt designs there.

Selling her company allowed Nancy the opportunity to focus on her passion for teaching at that time. She said, "I spent as much time as possible appliquéing and traveling and teaching others how easy and fun it is to do needle-turn appliqué, and how rewarding it is to make your very own Hawaiian-style quilt." Now that she has retired from teaching, she looks forward to spending more time on her own personal projects. "I now have time to continue my original mission to make a large Hawaiian quilt for each of my children!"

Nancy loves making her family quilts using significant motifs for each recipient. And she has a special method of choosing the kind of quilt it will be. She said, "Without asking each family member what they want, I spend time with them to learn about their likes (and dislikes) and choose a motif and design just for them.

I choose the color combination without asking them, because I need to love the fabric or I won't pick it up every day."

"All of my personal family quilts have stories about why I chose that flower or motif; and a couple of our patterns are very personal to me—Woodland Lei is all about the beauty of the Pacific Northwest forests and the changing of the colors in autumn; and Sea Turtles and Dolphins was created after I had an amazing snorkeling encounter with several sea turtles. Victorian Gingerbread was inspired by a piece of decorative woodwork on a house in Snohomish—I passed it every time I visited my sister."

For those who are interested in Hawaiian quilting, here's Nancy's seasoned advice: "You have to LIKE doing this, or you won't continue on getting better and better." When she first began quilting, her teacher encouraged her to find her own method, without thinking that there was only one correct way to quilt. Eventually, Nancy developed her own style of Hawaiian appliqué, or as she likes to call it, "The Chong way to appliqué." Nancy continued, "To be perfectly honest, I only know my own way of doing needle-turn applique—I have never taken a class from any other teacher. In the beginning, Luika Kamaka showed us how she used her needle to tuck under the seam allowance and how to stitch it in place; but after some time, I developed a style that worked better for me.

She encouraged me to pursue what I liked, not feel that I had to do it her way. I insisted that the beginners try it my way in class, but felt free to make adjustments to 'perfect' their own way of achieving a pleasing design."

Take a moment to slow down, try Hawaiian needle-turn applique, and see where it takes you. You might be surprised at how much you enjoy this traditional technique. Nancy herself never knew until she picked up a needle and thread. She said, "I experience joy and peace while making something by hand, using fabrics I chose, and bringing to life a design I created. My young daughter occasionally would hand me an applique project that I had set aside, and she'd say, 'Here, Mom, you need this right now.' And she was always right."

"It's easier than you can imagine, but you may need to try several techniques before you find the perfect one for you. And don't be afraid to mix ideas and techniques from several different teachers. If you see or can imagine a design that you HAVE to make, then you will have the incentive to seek out and find the book or teacher that will get you closer to your finished quilt." What motifs speak to you? What designs have you felt the urge to create? Just like Nancy, if you see a quilt that you can't forget, why not make it yourself? It could change everything.

How to Create a Quilter's Knot

Learning how to make a quilter's knot will save you time! Take the end of your thread and wrap it around the needle shaft about 3-4 times towards the point for a good-sized knot. Side the knot down the needle and the length of the thread until the end and cinch it tightly.

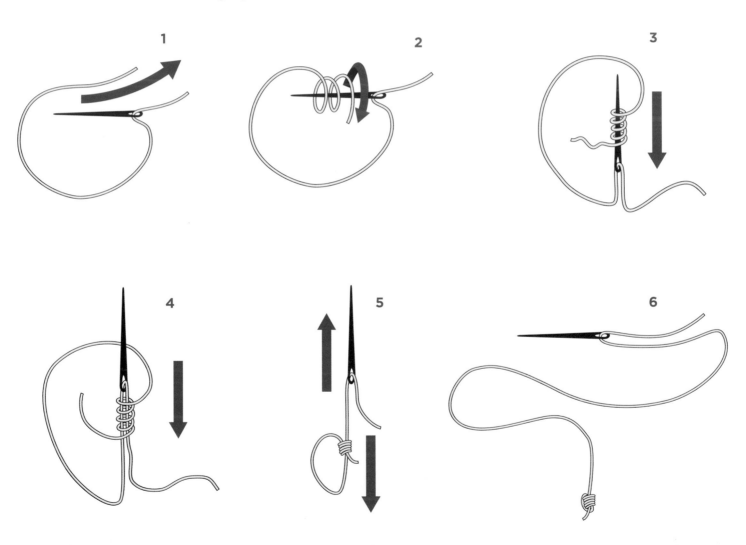

1

2

3

4

5

6

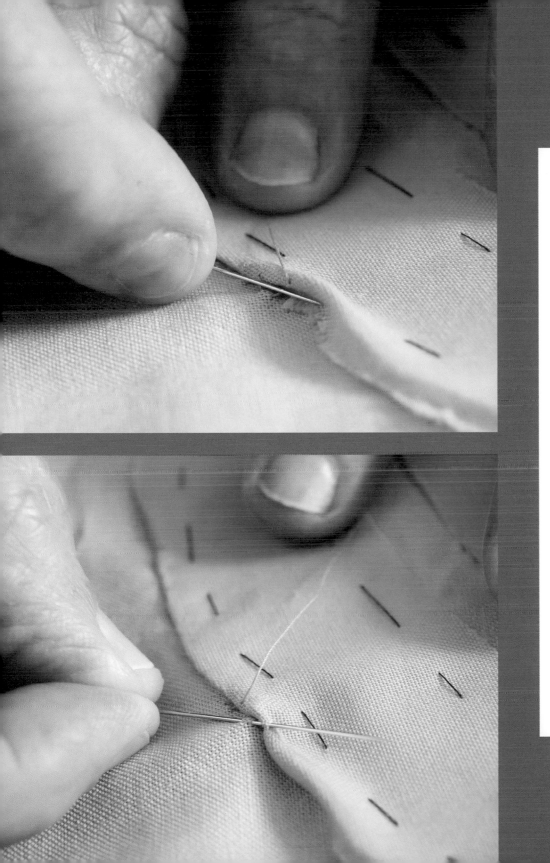

How to needle-turn

Needle-turn appliqué is achieved just like it sounds. The needle itself does the work. You use it to turn under the seam allowance, which is generally about ¼" or a bit less, and stitch the edge down with a blind stitch, also known as a ladder stitch.

How to make a blind stitch

A blind stitch or ladder stitch is a great way to appliqué. To begin, tie a quilter's knot and secure it under your appliqué design. Then, tuck a small section of your appliqué design about ¼" under with your needle. Push your needle up through the background fabric and appliqué design. Then, poke your needle back down into the background fabric, right below where your thread came out of the appliqué fabric, and create a small stitch that runs under the background fabric about an eighth of an inch or less (try to aim for 10 stitches per inch). The longer stitches will be hidden and only tiny stitches will be visible at the edge of your appliqué design. Again, push your needle back up through the folded edge of the appliqué design and continue on tucking the raw edge of the fabric under with your needle and stitching down the folded edge.

Look Toward the Sky
Skyward Quilt

For some, creativity appears to come naturally. Some say it's simply a trait, one people can't explain—some people seem to just get it and are naturally creative, while others must spend hours upon hours learning and mastering their craft. But either way, creativity is more than just a positive outlet for our thoughts and feelings. It's an energy that fills our entire beings and often manifests itself in the things we make and do.

But, where does this creative energy come from? Is it inside us? Or do we need to pay attention to it and grab it before it passes us by? Perhaps both. At times, inspiration and ideas seem to come from a completely different place millions of miles from here. These wonderful, out-of-the-blue ideas are like stars falling from the heavens. When we're in our crafting rooms and hear the whispers of a new creation, we can practically see the colors and unique designs as tiny specks in the starlit sky just outside our windows, blending into the constellations.

At first, ideas may come slowly, but then they grow bigger and become clearer, burning brightly as they barrel towards the earth—no, towards us. This is our opportunity to gather materials, find the perfect fabrics and complimenting color palettes, make measurements, and sketch out the pattern before the image burns too brightly for us to see it clearly. Then, the star vanishes, and we are left to admire the final product of our creative energy.

Just as a shooting star fills the sky with brilliance before hurtling to the earth only to burst into magnificent fragments, our ideas at times also seem to fall from the sky, moving quickly before they disappear, leaving behind a small crater in the back of our minds. We're convinced that we only have a tiny window to seize inspiration before it's replaced with something new that demands our attention. It's one of the minor burdens of having the creative mind of a quilter ... well, that and the accidental needle pricks to calloused fingers.

Sometimes we are inspired by the unique color combinations we see on early morning walks. Sometimes we get fun ideas for a quilt design while traveling to new places, browsing through favorite quilting books, or as we scroll through social media. Sometimes we can be so amazed by a piece of art or architecture that we have to find a way to incorporate the abstract movement of lines into a quilt using the fabrics from our overflowing scrap piles.

The best ideas come to us when we least expect them, and we have to seize the opportunities before they slip by us. So fellow quilters, we want to know—where do you find inspiration, or rather, how does inspiration find you? Do you also tend to look toward the sky?

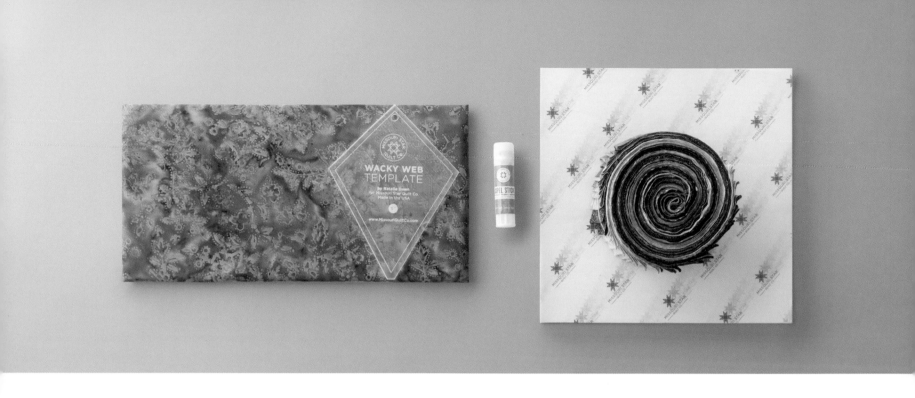

materials

QUILT SIZE
56½" x 56½"

BLOCK SIZE
10" unfinished, 9½" finished

QUILT TOP
1 roll of 2½" print strips
1½ yards of accent fabric
  - includes border

BINDING
½ yard

BACKING
3¾ yards - horizontal seam(s)

OTHER
Missouri Star Small Periwinkle
  (Wacky Web) Template for
  5" Charm Packs
1 package of Missouri Star
  10" Paper Piecing Squares
Water soluble glue stick or pen

SAMPLE QUILT
Lace & Grace Batiks
  by Island Batik

2A

1 cut & sort

From the accent fabric:

- Cut (4) 5″ strips across the width of the fabric. Using the template, subcut 8 periwinkles from each of 3 strips. Cut 1 additional periwinkle from the remaining strip for a **total of 25**.

- Cut the remainder of the strip lengthwise into (2) 2½″ strips and add these to your roll of strips.

- Set the remaining fabric aside for the border.

Select 9 *pairs* of matching 2½″ print strips from your roll of strips. Cut the selected strips into 2½″ x 11½″ rectangles. Organize the rectangles into a **total of 25** matching pairs. **Notes**: You will have 1 rectangle left over. If your roll of strips does not have enough matching strips, you can either cut more strips from the accent fabric, or pair similar strips for your quilt.

2 block construction

Tips: These blocks use a paper piecing method. Set your machine stitch length to 2.0 mm or shorter to prevent tearing out stitches when you remove the paper. It is helpful to have a small cutting mat, rotary cutter, small ironing mat, and iron close to your sewing machine.

Fold each 10″ paper square in half, once on the diagonal, and crease to mark the center. Fold each periwinkle in half along the length and crease to mark the center. **2A**

Apply a small amount of glue to the reverse side of the periwinkle and adhere it to the paper square, right side up, as shown. Use the marked centerlines to position your periwinkle. **2B**

Select a print strip and cut a 2½″ x 6½″ rectangle. Lay the rectangle, face down, atop the glued periwinkle as shown. Be sure the outside corner is slightly past the edge of the paper. Sew along the edge using a ¼″ seam allowance. **2C**

Open and press. **2D**

From the same strip, cut a 2½″ x 9″ rectangle. Set the remainder of the strip aside for the moment.* Lay the rectangle, face down, atop the glued periwinkle as shown. Again, the outside corner is just past the edge of the paper. Sew along the edge as before. **2E**

*__Note__: Set the remainder of the print strip aside for the moment. Each print strip is long enough to make 2 rows. Open and press. **2F**

Select a different print strip and cut a 2½″ x 9½″ rectangle. In the same manner, lay the rectangle face down, line up the edges, and sew along the edge. **2G**

Open and press. **2H**

Repeat to cut a 2½″ x 11½″ rectangle from the same strip and add it to the opposite side. **2I**

2B    **2C**

2D 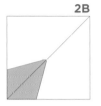   **2E**

2F    **2G**

2H   **2I**

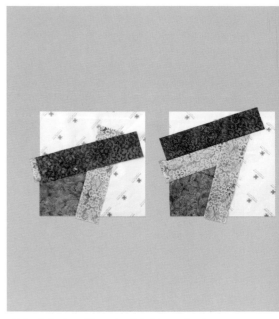

1 Glue a periwinkle to the paper square, right side up, as shown. Select a print strip and cut a 2½" x 6½" rectangle. Lay the rectangle, face down, atop the glued periwinkle as shown. Sew along the edge using a ¼" seam allowance. Open and press.

2 From the same print strip, cut a 2½" x 9" rectangle. Lay the rectangle, face down, atop the glued periwinkle as shown. Sew along the edge as before. Open and press.

3 Select a different print strip and cut a 2½" x 9½" rectangle. In the same manner, lay the rectangle face down, line up the edges, and sew along the edge. Open and press.

4 Repeat to cut a 2½" x 11½" rectangle from the same strip and add it to the opposite side. Select a pair of matching 2½" x 11½" print rectangles and sew 1 to either side.

5 From a print strip, trim (2) 2½" x 1" rectangles and add 1 to either corner.

6 Turn the block over and trim along the edges of the paper square. Carefully remove the paper backing from your block.

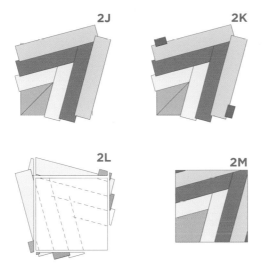

2J   **2K**

2L   **2M**

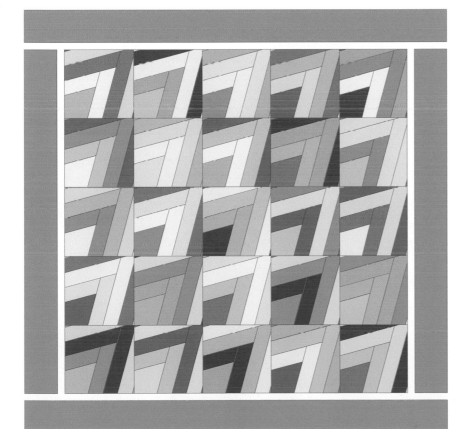

Select a pair of matching 2½" x 11½" print rectangles and sew 1 to either side. **2J**

From a print strip, trim (2) 2½" x 1" rectangles and add 1 to either corner. **2K**

Turn the block over and trim along the edges of the paper square. **2L**

Note: If your paper has "shrunk", you can use a 10" ruler to trim to 10" square. Carefully remove the paper backing from your block. **Make 25**. **2M**

Block Size: 10" unfinished, 9½" finished

3 arrange & sew

Refer to the diagram on the left to lay out your units in **5 rows of 5**. Sew the blocks together in rows. Press the seams in opposite directions. Nest the seams and sew the rows together. Press.

4 border

Cut (5) 5" strips across the width of the outer border fabric. Sew the strips together to make 1 long strip. Trim the borders from this strip. Refer to Borders (pg. 118) in the Construction Basics to measure, cut, and attach the borders. The lengths are approximately 48" for the sides and 57" for the top and bottom.

5 quilt & bind

Layer the quilt with batting and backing, then quilt. See Construction Basics (pg. 118) to add binding and finish your quilt.

For Auld Lang Syne
Candy Lane Quilt

As the year draws to a close, many of us prepare to throw one of the longest parties ever. After all, a New Year's party starts in one year and doesn't end until the next! Whether your plans involve a big blow-out celebration watching the Times Square Ball drop with fireworks, or just a quiet evening of sewing and sitting with loved ones and a kiss at midnight, everybody has their own special traditions to ring in the New Year right.

The one tradition we all like to take part in (or at least watch on TV) is the ball dropping in Times Square. Which, if you think about it, is kind of an odd tradition. What does a large metal sphere covered in lights have to do with the ending of the calendar? Well, it's a bit ambiguous as to where it comes from, but some suggest it is tied to maritime timekeeping, where a land-based mechanism would drop balls at predetermined times that you could set your ship's clock to, so you would have an accurate account of time on the high seas!

In the South and parts of the Midwest, one tradition is to eat a bowl of "Hoppin' John" for dinner before the New Year begins. Savory bacon and black eyed peas get mixed with spinach or collard greens and rice into a delicious and filling bowl of goodness, served with a generous portion of sweet cornbread.

It's definitely a tasty Southern comfort food, but why is this tradition so common? The way I was told about the tradition said that the black-eyed peas represent coins, with the spinach being dollar bills, and the cornbread standing in for gold bars. They say that ending the year with these symbols for wealth encourages prosperity in the year to come! Whether or not it works, it sure is a tasty way to celebrate. They have a similar dish in Italy that they eat at the same time, except it replaces slices of sausage to represent the coins.

As for the kissing, that is actually believed to come from ancient German and Scandinavian traditions, where the first person you see in the New Year will be impactful on the following twelve months. So, why not take it into your own hands and make sure it's someone you love? Plus, there's worse ways to end and begin a year than embracing your favorite person in the world!

What are your favorite ways to ring in the New Year? Write to us on Facebook or at blockstories@missouriquiltco.com and share your traditions to treasure the memories of the old, and embrace the dreams of the new.

materials

QUILT SIZE
70" x 70"

BLOCK SIZE
10" unfinished, 9½" finished

QUILT TOP
1 roll of 2½" print strips
1 roll of 1½" background strips
 - includes inner border

OUTER BORDER
1¼ yards

BINDING
¾ yard

BACKING
4½ yards - vertical seam(s)
   or 2¼ yards of 108" wide

OTHER
1 package of Missouri Star
   10" Paper Piecing Squares
Water soluble glue stick or pen

SAMPLE QUILT
**Kaffe Fassett Collective
- August 2021 Bright Colorway**
   by Kaffe Fassett for FreeSpirit
   Fabrics

1 make strip sets

Sort the 2½" print strips into 5 sets of 6 different strips and 3 sets of 3 different strips.

Sew 1 set of 6 print strips together lengthwise. Press. **Make 5**. Cut each strip set into 2½" segments. A **total of 72** long pieced strips are needed. **1A**

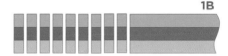

Take the remaining segments apart at the seams to **make (72)** 2½" squares.

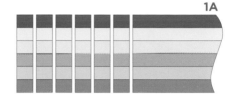

Sew 1 set of 3 print strips together lengthwise. Press. **Make 3**. Cut each strip set into 1½" segments. A **total of 72** short pieced strips are needed. **1B**

2 block construction

Tips: These blocks use a paper piecing method. Set your machine stitch length to 2.0 mm or shorter to prevent tearing out stitches when you remove the paper. It is helpful to have a small cutting mat, rotary cutter, small ironing mat, and iron close to your sewing machine.

Set (6) 1½" background strips aside for the inner border. **Note**: You will use (1) 1½" background strip per block.

Select a 1½" background strip and cut a 1½" x 14½" rectangle from the strip. Apply a small amount of glue corner to corner once across the paper and adhere the rectangle to the paper, right side up. **Note**: Be careful not to stretch the fabric. **2A**

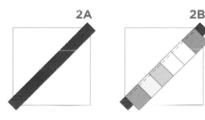

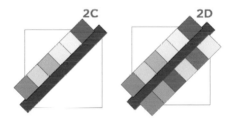

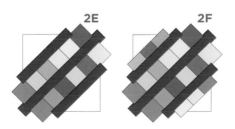

Lay a long pieced strip, face down, atop the glued background strip and line up the edges as shown. Sew along the edge using a ¼" seam allowance. **2B**

Open and press. **2C**

Repeat to add a different long pieced strip to the opposite side of the background strip and press. **2D**

Cut (2) 1½" x 9" rectangles from the background strip. In the same manner, add these rectangles to the block and press. **2E**

Next, add 2 different short pieced strips—1 to each side of the outer background rectangles and press. **2F**

Cut (2) 1½" x 4½" rectangles from the background strip. Add them to either side of the short pieced strips and press. **2G**

Add a 2½" print square to either side of the outer background rectangles and press. **2H**

Turn the unit over and trim along the edges of the paper square. **2I**

Carefully remove the paper backing from your block. **Make 36**. **2J**

Block Size: 10" unfinished, 9½" finished

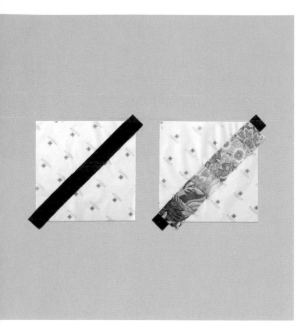
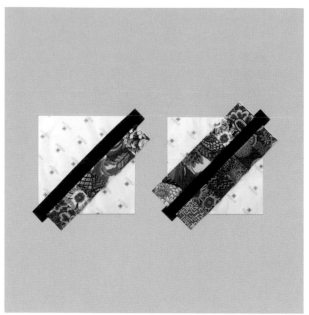

1 Apply a small amount of glue corner to corner once across the paper and adhere the background rectangle to the paper, right side up. Lay a long pieced strip, face down, atop the background strip, lining up the edges. Sew along the edge using a ¼" seam allowance.

2 Open and press. Repeat to add a different long pieced strip to the opposite side of the background strip and press.

3 Cut (2) 1½" x 9" rectangles from the background strip. In the same manner, add these rectangles to the block and press. Next, add 2 different short pieced strips—1 to each side of the outer background rectangles and press.

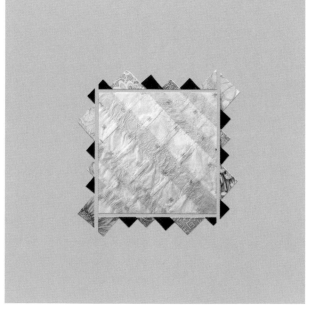

4 Cut (2) 1½" x 4½" rectangles from the background strip. Add them to either side of the short pieced strips and press. Add a 2½" print square to either side of the outer background rectangles and press.

5 Turn the unit over and trim along the edges of the paper square. Carefully remove the paper backing from your block. Make 36.

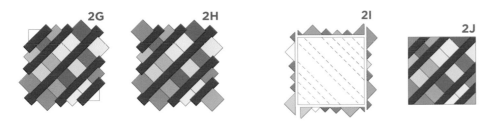

2G   2H   2I   2J

3 arrange & sew

Refer to the diagram below to lay out your units in **6 rows of 6**. Notice that the diagonals within the blocks alternate, creating background diamonds. Sew the blocks together in rows. Press the seams in opposite directions. Nest the seams and sew the rows together. Press.

4 inner border

Sew the (6) 1½" strips together to make 1 long strip. Trim the borders from this strip. Refer to Borders (pg. 118) in the Construction Basics to measure, cut, and attach the borders. The strip lengths are approximately 57½" for the sides and 59½" for the top and bottom.

5 outer border

Cut (7) 6" strips across the width of the outer border fabric. Sew the strips together to make 1 long strip. Trim the borders from this strip. Refer to Borders (pg. 118) in the Construction Basics to measure, cut, and attach the borders. The lengths are approximately 59½" for the sides and 70½" for the top and bottom.

6 quilt & bind

Layer the quilt with batting and backing, then quilt. See Construction Basics (pg. 118) to add binding and finish your quilt.

Welcome Color into Your Home
Flower Chain Quilt

Even though there's plenty to love and enjoy during winter, like hot chocolate, sledding, and more time to sew, it can still be difficult to see those flowers (and warm weather) go. But there's good news and bad news. The bad news is we can't have snowball fights in 80 degree weather, and the good news is you can still have flowers and bright colors in a winter wonderland! When you're a quilter, you will never be without color, and the staying-indoors season is prime sewing time. If you have fabric (of course), thread, and a sewing machine, then you have everything you need to keep your home colorful! We all know how far and between sunny days can be in winter, which makes it hard to get cheerful daylight into the house. But the lack of sunshine-filled afternoons is the perfect reason to unpack that overflowing stash of floral fabric we know you've got!

Like we said, quilters lead colorful lives, so you could easily color your home with something as simple as a couch throw or table runner made with beautiful red poppies, roses, or any of your favorite floral prints from your stash. Such a splash of color would make you forget all about those pesky gray clouds crowding the sky! And when your stash and sewing machine can only take you so far, that's when you pay a visit to the Christmas section at your local crafts store. When you think of flowers during winter, you probably see extravagant red and white poinsettias, but they aren't the only artificial flowers you can find blooming in the Christmas section. Artificial bouquets and centerpieces of roses mixed in with winterberry, pine cones, and other merry flowers are surprisingly easy to come by, which means you can keep your home looking like a merry and bright garden all season long!

And you don't have to stop there. Unless you're a botanist or an avid gardener, you may not know that there are breeds of flowers that can actually survive cold climates. Yes, it's true! You can have flowers indoors and outdoors! Aside from obvious plants like winterberry holly and spring snowflakes, there is a surprising number of flowers that can handle Jack Frost. Take daffodils for example! Have you ever noticed that these beautiful yellow blooms tend to pop up at the tail end of winter? Not only are they a very welcoming first sign of spring, they're able to sprout as early as February because of their cold hardy nature. So if those gray winter skies tend to get you down in the dumps, "plant" ahead and stock up on daffodil bulbs! If you live in a region where your winters are on the mild side, another cold-hardy flower you could keep in your garden is the pansy. These vibrant flowers can tough out light frosts, and with your tender love and care, they will bloom bright for you all winter long.

So, what do you think? Feeling less sad about autumns's end? We don't blame you if you're still not ready to say goodbye to the warmer weather, we're all going to miss it! But now you know you at least don't have to be without flowers come winter, indoors or out! For such a simple pleasure, flowers have a remarkable ability to lift our spirits and put smiles on faces, and everyone deserves to smile as much as possible. So don't let Jack Frost or cloudy skies keep you from having the things that make you smile, whether it's with fabric, seasonal decorations, or a pack of seeds.

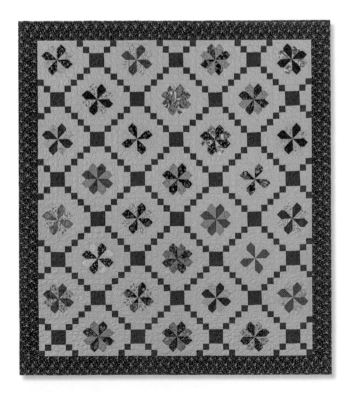

materials

QUILT SIZE
75½" x 85"

BLOCK SIZE
10" unfinished, 9½" finished

QUILT TOP
3 packages of 5" print squares
1¼ yards of accent fabric
4½ yards of background fabric

BORDER
1¼ yards

BINDING
¾ yard

BACKING
5¼ yards - vertical seam(s)
   or 2¾ yards of 108" wide

OPTIONAL
Clearly Perfect Slotted Trimmer A
Missouri Star 10" Square Template

SAMPLE QUILT
Moonstone by Laundry Basket
   Quilts for Andover Fabric,
Bella Solids - Blush
   by Moda Fabrics,
Kona Cotton - Silver
   by Robert Kaufman Fabrics

2A

2B

2C

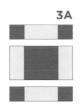

3A

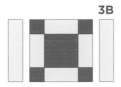

3B

1 cut

From the accent fabric, cut (3) 4" strips and (12) 2" strips across the width of the fabric.

From the background fabric, cut:

- (3) 7" strips across the width of the fabric.

- (3) 4" strips across the width of the fabric.

- (7) 2½" strips across the width of the fabric. Subcut a **total of (112)** 2½" squares.

- (16) 2" strips across the width of the fabric. Subcut 10 strips into a **total of (56)** 2" x 7" rectangles.

- (19) 1¾" strips across the width of the fabric. Subcut a **total of (448)** 1¾" squares.

- (28) 1½" strips across the width of the fabric. Subcut 14 strips into a **total of (56)** 1½" x 10½" rectangles. Subcut the other 14 strips into a **total of (56)** 1½" x 8½" rectangles.

2 make units

Sew a 2" background strip to the top and bottom of a 4" accent strip. Press towards the darker fabric. **Make 3**. Cut these strip sets into 4" increments to create a **total of 28** A units. **2A**

Sew a 2" accent strip to the top and bottom of a 4" background strip. Press towards the darker fabric. **Make 3**. Cut these strip sets into 2" increments to create a **total of 56** B units. **2B**

Sew a 2" accent strip to the top and bottom of a 7" background strip. Press the seams toward the background fabric. **Make 3**. Cut these strip sets into 2" increments to create a **total of 56** C units. **2C**

3 chain block construction

Lay 1 A unit and 2 B units in 3 rows as shown. Nest the seams and sew the rows together to complete the block center. **3A**

Sew a 2" x 7" background rectangle to either side of the block center. Press the seams toward the outside edges. **3B**

Sew a C unit to the top and bottom of the center unit, nesting the seams as you go. Press. **Make 28**. **3C 3D**

Block Size: 10" unfinished, 9½" finished

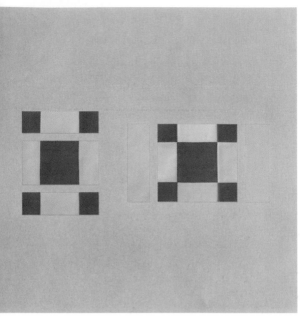

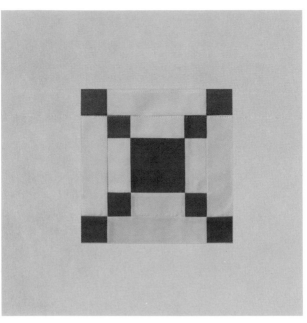

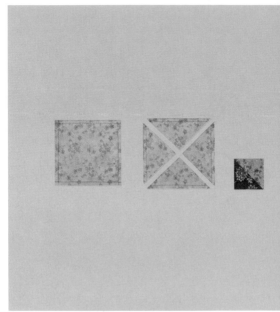

1 Lay 1 A unit and 2 B units in 3 rows as shown. Nest the seams and sew the rows together to complete the block center. Sew a 2" x 7" background rectangle to either side of the block center. Press the seams toward the outside edges.

2 Sew a C unit to the top and bottom of the center unit, nesting the seams as you go. Press.

3 Lay 2 unmatching 5" print squares together, right sides facing. Sew around the perimeter. Cut the sewn squares twice diagonally. Square each unit to 2½". Each set of sewn squares will yield 4 half-square triangles.

4 Arrange the 4 half-square triangles in a pinwheel as shown. Sew the units together in 2 rows and press in opposite directions. Sew the rows together, then press to complete the pinwheel.

5 Place a 1¾" marked background square on 1 corner of a 2½" print square, right sides facing. Sew on the marked line. Trim the excess fabric away. Press open. Repeat with another 1¾" marked background square to snowball an adjacent corner.

6 Arrange (4) 2½" background squares, 4 petal units, and the pinwheel in 3 rows of 3 as shown. Sew the units together in rows and press in opposite directions. Nest the seams and sew the rows together. Press.

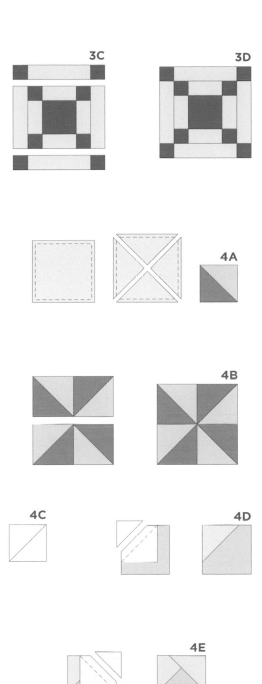

3C

3D

4A

4B

4C

4D

4E

4 flower block construction

Select 56 pairs of matching prints and set the remaining squares aside for another project.

Select 2 different pairs of 5″ print squares. Lay 2 non-matching 5″ print squares together, right sides facing. Sew around the perimeter. Cut the sewn squares twice diagonally. Use trimmer A to square each unit to 2½″, then press open—or press, then square to 2½″ if you're not using the trimmer. Each set of sewn squares will yield 4 half-square triangles. **4A**

Arrange the 4 half-square triangles in a pinwheel as shown. Sew the units together in 2 rows and press in opposite directions. Sew the rows together, then press to complete the pinwheel. **4B**

Cut the other 2 selected 5″ print squares in half vertically and horizontally to create (4) 2½″ squares of each print.

Mark a line from corner to corner on the reverse side of each 1¾″ background square. **4C**

Place a 1¾″ marked background square on 1 corner of a 2½″ print square, right sides facing. Sew on the marked line. Trim the excess fabric away ¼″ from the sewn seam. Press open. **4D**

Repeat with another 1¾" marked
background square to snowball an
adjacent corner. Snowball 2 adjacent
corners of each of the 2½" print squares
to **make 2** sets of 4 matching petals. **4E**

Sew a petal of each print side by side as
shown. **Note**: Reference **4G** as needed
to make sure that the order of the prints
in your petals will match the pinwheel.
Make 4 petal units. **4F**

Arrange (4) 2½" background squares,
4 petal units, and the pinwheel in 3 rows
of 3 as shown. Sew the units together in
rows and press in opposite directions.
Nest the seams and sew the rows
together. Press. **4G**

Sew a 1½" x 8½" rectangle to either side
of the unit you just made. Press towards
the rectangles. Sew a 1½" x 10½"
rectangle to the top and bottom of
the unit. Press towards the rectangles.
Use the square template and align
the centerline with the center seams or
measure 5" from the center seams and
trim the block to 10" square. **Make 28**.
4H 4I

Block Size: 10" unfinished, 9½" finished

4F

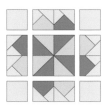

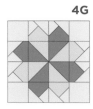

4G

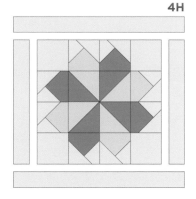

4H

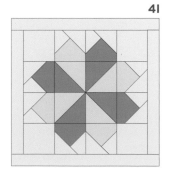

4I

5 arrange & sew

Refer to the diagram on the left as necessary to lay out your units in **8 rows of 7 blocks**. Notice that the first row begins with a flower block and alternates with chain blocks from there. Sew the blocks together in rows. Press the seams in opposite directions. Nest the seams and sew the rows together. Press.

6 border

Cut (8) 5" strips across the width of the border fabric. Sew the strips together to make 1 long strip. Trim the borders from this strip. Refer to Borders (pg. 118) in the Construction Basics to measure, cut, and attach the borders. The strip lengths are approximately 76½" for the sides and 76" for the top and bottom.

7 quilt & bind

Layer the quilt with batting and backing, then quilt. See Construction Basics (pg. 118) to add binding and finish your quilt.

Style is in His DNA

Christopher Thompson

Christopher Thompson was born in a small, southwestern Virginia town surrounded by makers. His great-grandmother, Mary, was a quilter and dressmaker. His grandmother, Elizabeth, and several of his great-aunts were also quilters. You could say being a maker was going to be part of his DNA, because both of his parents, Cecil and Jackie, were makers as well. He said, "My dad was quite the carpenter and my mother loved any kind of trendy craft like scrapbooking, and was also quite talented at crochet and knitting." It's easy to see where his design savvy originated.

Currently, you'll find him hard at work as the Director of Product Marketing for Riley Blake Designs. He is the link between the marketing and design teams, creating new and fresh marketing ideas for their beautiful fabrics and innovative products. In addition, he leads their talented graphic design team and works closely with their Sourcing Manager to develop and launch new notions and products for Riley Blake Designs and their awesome roster of designers. He also partners with Riley Blake's Creative Director and Design Director on new fabric releases.

When we asked Christopher to talk about his style as a quilter, he said, "I would describe myself as a modern-traditional quilter. The foundation of my quilting style is traditional with a modern spin. My style continues to evolve and I've recently discovered I go through phases."

"While my quilting style is modern-traditional, my fabric designs sway more traditional. They're grounded in florals, geometrics, and often in a blue color palette (blue is one of my favorite colors). The first mini quilt I made featured shades of blue, a traditional quilt block, and was entirely pieced on a machine and hand quilted by me at the age of 15. I made it for a church talent competition where I was teased for making something that was typically made by a female. I've tried throughout my quilting journey to identify as a 'quilter' versus a 'male quilter.' My gender has nothing to do with my work as a quilter."

The quilt that Christopher designed especially for BLOCK is called "Jewel." We asked him, "What is the inspiration behind the quilt you designed for BLOCK?" He said, "I started designing Jewel with the intention of taking traditional quilt blocks and giving them a modern spin through unique color combinations and placement. If you look closely, you'll see there are more than just two traditional blocks in this quilt." His fabulous Jewel quilt design features a background of almost neutral teal greens with pops of fuchsia, pink, yellow, and light blue—an unlikely color combination that absolutely works.

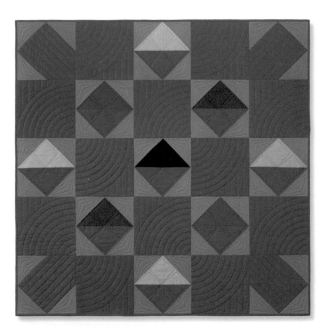

materials

QUILT SIZE
50" x 50"

BLOCK SIZE
10½" unfinished, 10" finished

QUILT TOP
¼ yard blue solid*
¼ yard pink solid*
¼ yard fuschia solid*
¼ yard yellow solid*
1 yard aqua solid
2 yards teal solid

BINDING
½ yard

BACKING
3¼ yards - horizontal seam(s)

*__Note__: Fat quarters may be
   substituted for the ¼ yard cuts.

SAMPLE QUILT
Confetti Cottons by Riley Blake
   Pieced by Christopher Thompson

2A

2B

2C

2D

1 cut

From each of the blue and pink fabrics, cut (1) 5½" strip across the width of the fabric. Subcut (2) 5½" x 10½" rectangles.

From the fuschia fabric, cut (1) 5½" strip across the width of the fabric. Subcut (1) 5½" x 10½" rectangle.

From the yellow fabric, cut (1) 5½" strip across the width of the fabric. Subcut (4) 5½" x 10½" rectangles.

From the teal fabric, cut (6) 10½" strips across the width of the fabric. From 4 strips, subcut a **total of (16)** 10½" squares. From 2 strips, subcut a **total of (9)** 10½" x 5½" rectangles.

From the aqua fabric, cut (7) 5½" strips across the width of the fabric. Subcut a **total of (48)** 5½" squares.

3A

2 sew flying geese

Draw a diagonal line on the reverse side of the 5½" aqua squares. Set 12 marked squares aside for section 4. **2A**

With right sides together, place 1 aqua square atop the right edge of a yellow rectangle as shown. Sew on the line. Trim ¼" beyond the seam. Press the aqua fabric back to make a new corner. **2B**

Stack another 5½" aqua square atop the left edge of the rectangle. Sew on the line. Trim ¼" beyond the seam and press the aqua fabric back to make a new corner. **Make 4** yellow flying geese units. **2C**

Repeat the steps to create the following flying geese units: **make 2** pink, **make 1** fuchsia, **make 2** blue, and **make 9** teal. **2D**

3 make flying geese diamonds

Arrange a yellow flying geese unit and teal flying geese unit, as shown. Sew the flying geese units together and press towards the teal. **3A**

Block Size: 10½" unfinished, 10" finished

Repeat to sew each remaining yellow, pink, fuchsia, and blue flying geese unit to a teal flying geese unit.

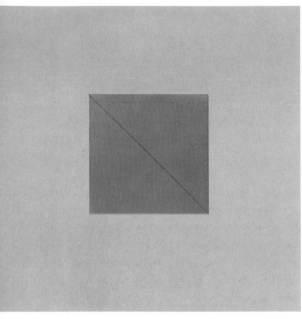

1 Draw a diagonal line on the reverse side of the 5½″ aqua squares.

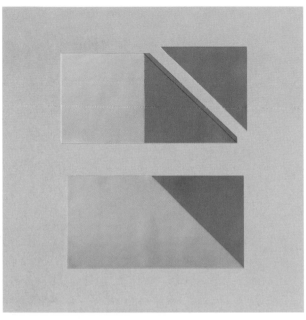

2 With right sides together, place 1 aqua square atop the right edge of a yellow rectangle as shown. Sew on the line. Trim ¼″ beyond the seam. Press the aqua fabric back to make a new corner.

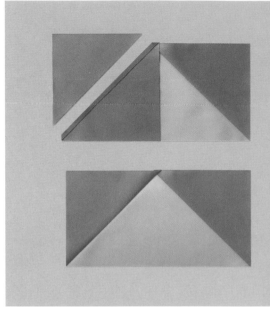

3 Lay another 5½″ aqua square atop the left edge of the rectangle. Sew on the line. Trim ¼″ beyond the seam and press the aqua fabric back to make a new corner.

4 Arrange a yellow flying geese unit and teal flying geese unit, as shown. Sew the flying geese units together and press towards the teal.

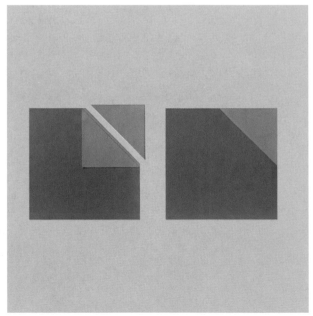

5 Lay a marked aqua square, right sides facing, on the top right corner of a 10½″ teal square as shown. Sew on the line. Trim ¼″ beyond the seam and press the aqua fabric back to make a new corner.

6 In the same manner, add another aqua corner to the top left, then bottom left of the teal square.

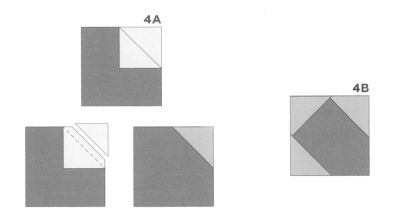

4A

4B

4 make corner blocks

Lay a marked aqua square, right sides facing, on the top right corner of a 10½" teal square as shown. Sew on the line. Trim ¼" beyond the seam and press the aqua fabric back to make a new corner. **4A**

In the same manner, add another aqua corner to the top left, then bottom left of the teal square. **Make 4** corner blocks. **4B**

Block Size: 10½" unfinished, 10" finished

5 arrange & sew

Arrange the flying geese diamonds, corner blocks, and 10½" teal squares into **5 rows of 5** as shown in the diagram on the left. Sew the blocks together to form rows. Press the seams toward the teal squares. Nest the seams and sew the rows together. Press.

6 quilt & bind

Layer the quilt with batting and backing, then quilt. After the quilting is complete, see Construction Basics (pg. 118) to add binding and finish your quilt.

Family Treasures
Four-Patch Tumbler Quilt

By Janet Meleney, a customer story

The first quilter I know of in my family was my great, great grandmother Eliza Ann (Innis) Meleney, 1826-1908, originally of Salem, Mass. She was the oldest of 12 children born to John Ashley Innis and Eliza Phelps. Eliza Ann was the wife and widow of Henry Edmund Meleney of Cape Breton, Canada. They were the parents of at least 8 children, only 3 of whom lived to be adults and only one who married and had children. Now there are 6 generations of descendants who honor her legacy. As the family historian, I keep a list of all the descendants, addresses, comings and goings, and update it yearly for all. I was also lucky enough to be the inheritor of many family assets and am now making sure that these treasures and their stories get passed down to the younger generations.

Among these treasures was a box of Victorian crazy quilt squares made by the widow Eliza Ann Innis Meleney in the 1880s. Each square is composed of scraps of dress material and ribbons mounted on muslin, embroidered and embellished as was the custom of the day. Some of the squares have her notes on the back of the date and where she was or who she was with. The 54 completed or partially completed squares were never sewn into a whole quilt, but stored away in her son's attic until I inherited them in 1980. I decided that the silks and satins were much too fragile for use and would survive better if displayed and shared. I started getting individual squares framed, with archival matting, and giving them to cousins when they got married. Each gift was accompanied by a photo and genealogical information on EAIM. In more recent days the cost of framing for so many cousins has gotten out of hand, but I still give them to those interested, as well as instructions on matting and framing the square.

The second quilt that inspired me as an adult, was an alphabet quilt that had been made for my mother, Elaine (Kolster) Meleney, 1920-1994, by her cousin Adele (Kolster) Goetz, 1896-1972. I do not know if it was given to her when she was a child or perhaps as a wedding present. When my brother and I were little, this quilt was taken out only for special occasions such as holidays, birthdays, or when we needed a little extra comfort. I know for sure that it was thrown up on multiple times. My mother gave it to me when she downsized to senior living. When my mother was in assisted living and needed a little extra comfort, I returned it to her. She loved the thought but told me she didn't want it ruined. Would I please make her her own quilt for her single bed, in pinks and blues, that could be sat on and washed in the facility laundry room. And that is how I started making quilts. Incidentally, my first class was a quilt in a day log cabin class, much like Jenny!

materials

QUILT SIZE
43½" x 53½"

BLOCK SIZE
5" unfinished tumbler,
4½" finished tumbler

QUILT TOP
1 package of 5" print squares
¾ yard of background fabric
  - includes inner border
½ yard of accent fabric

OUTER BORDER
1 yard

BINDING
½ yard

BACKING
3 yards - horizontal seam(s)

OTHER
Missouri Star Small Tumbler
  Template for 5" Charm Packs

SAMPLE QUILT
Mary Ann's Gift 1850-1880
  by Betsy Chutchian
  for Moda Fabrics

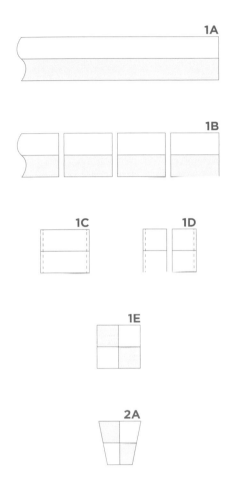

1A

1B

1C   1D

1E

2A

1 make the four-patches

From the background and accent fabrics, cut (6) 2¾" strips across the width of each fabric. Set the remainder of the background fabric aside for the inner border.

Sew a background strip to an accent strip, lengthwise. Open and press. **Make 6**. **1A**

Trim each strip set into (7) 5" x 5½" units. **1B**

Place 2 units 1 atop the other with right sides facing and opposite fabrics touching. Sew along both shorter sides, perpendicular to the previously sewn seam. **1C**

Cut the sewn units in the center, parallel to the 2 seams you have just sewn. Open and press each unit. **Make 42** and then set 1 unit aside for another project. **1D 1E**

2 cut

Select (2) 5" print squares from your package and set them aside for another project. Use the template to cut a tumbler from each remaining print square. A **total of 40** are needed.

Select a 4-patch unit and rotate it so the accent fabric is in the upper left corner. Place the template on top of the unit and cut a tumbler shape. Repeat to cut a **total of 41**. **2A**

Block Size: 5" unfinished tumbler, 4½" finished tumbler

3 arrange & sew

Refer to the diagram on page 55 to layout the blocks in **9 rows of 9**. Notice how the different tumblers alternate with 1 another. Sew the blocks together to form the rows. Press in the rows in opposite directions. Nest the seams and sew the rows together. Press. **3A**

Place an acrylic ruler on the sides of your quilt top, connecting the inner part of the jagged sides. Trim the jagged edges of the sides of the quilt top so it is now a rectangle. Your quilt top will be approximately 31" wide. **3B**

1 Sew a 2¾" background strip to a 2¾" accent strip, lengthwise. Open and press towards the accent fabric. Make 6 strip sets.

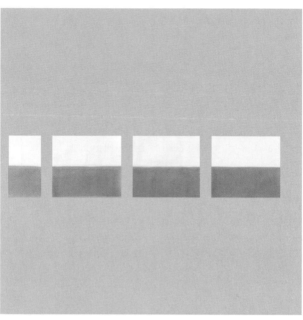

2 Cut each strip set into (7) 5" x 5½" units.

3 Place 2 units right sides together with opposite fabrics touching and seams nested. Sew together along the short sides, perpendicular to the previously sewn seams.

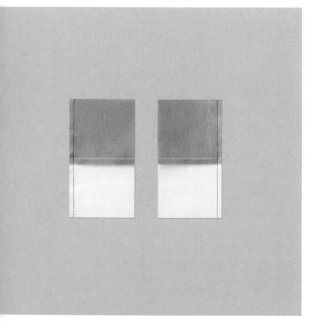

4 Cut the sewn unit in the center, parallel to the 2 seams you just sewed.

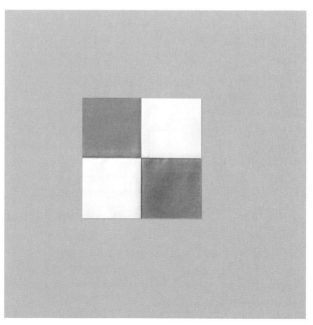

5 Open and press each unit.

6 Rotate a 4-patch unit as shown, then place the template on top. Be sure the template is centered on the unit, then cut around it to yield a 4-patch tumbler. Make a total of (41) 4-patch tumblers.

3A

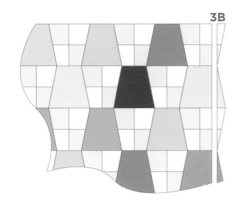

3B

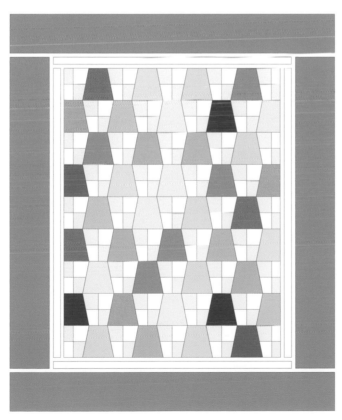

4 inner border

From the background fabric, cut (4) 1½" strips across the width of the fabric. Cut the inner borders from these strips. Refer to Borders (pg. 118) in the Construction Basics to measure, cut, and attach the borders. The strip lengths are approximately 41" for the sides and 33" for the top and bottom.

5 outer border

From the outer border fabric, cut (5) 6" strips* across the width of the fabric. Sew the strips together to form 1 long strip. Cut the outer borders from this strip. Refer to Borders (pg. 118) in the Construction Basics to measure, cut, and attach the borders. The strip lengths are approximately 43" for the sides and 44" for the top and bottom.

*__Note__: You may be able to cut the border strips from 4 individual strips without sewing them together. Measure your quilt top and the width of your fabric. If the width of fabric is more than the width of the quilt top, you can cut the borders from 4 individual strips without sewing them together first.

6 quilt & bind

Layer the quilt with batting and backing, then quilt. See Construction Basics (pg. 118) to add binding and finish your quilt.

Mistakes are Proof You're Trying

Everyone makes mistakes, even quilters! I like to remember the quote, "Mistakes are proof that you're trying," and repeat it to myself often. Every time I try something new, and even when I've done something many times before, I expect to pull out my seam ripper. It's such an essential sewing notion. I often find myself "frog sewing," as I like to call it: Rip it! Rip it! But instead of seeing seam ripping as a mistake, I like to see it as a part of sewing and an opportunity to learn. After all, pencils come with erasers attached! Nobody expects you to write without making corrections, so how can we expect ourselves to sew without making corrections? Seam rippers are our erasers as we simply are not perfect people.

If you take a peek inside the little tool storage box that comes either attached to or alongside your sewing machine, you're going to find a few items, including a tiny seam ripper. The seam ripper that comes with your sewing machine is usually fine in a pinch, but tends to be too small to hold comfortably and is often dull from years of use. It's time to level up and make seam ripping less of a chore. It can be easy with the right tool used in the right way.

Ready to Roll
Get rid of those pesky bits of thread left over from seam ripping quickly and easily with a lint roller! They're a must-have tool for every sewing room. And be sure to give yourself a once-over too; there's bound to be a few threads stuck to your pants!

Here are a few of our favorite seam rippers. They're great for everyday use, travel, and some even come with lights and magnifying glasses attached to them. Which one do you prefer?

Classic
The white Clover seam ripper is a perennial favorite among quilters. With an easy to grip handle and a sharp blade, it's simple to use and easy to love.

Multifunctional
The Seam-Fix Tool is amazing for multitasking. One side is a seam ripper and the other side is a fine rounded tip awl that can also be used as a stiletto. The thread eraser cap rubs stray threads away easily.

Adaptive
For those who have trouble gripping a seam ripper, or enjoy a hands-free option, the Fiskars Tabletop Seam Ripper provides a faster, less stressful way to rip seams. The powerful suction cup attaches to your work surface, allowing you to keep both hands on your project.

The Mighty Bright LED Lighted seam ripper comes with a magnifier to help you see the smallest stitches with ease by quadrupling the image size of your blade and stitch.

Precise
It's no surprise that Havels makes surgical instruments as well as sewing notions. The Havels Seam Ripper Ultra Pro is like a scalpel for removing stitches with precision, and it comes with replaceable blades to keep your seam ripper sharp.

Cindy's seam ripper is ergonomic, meant to fit right on the tip of your pointer finger or middle finger for precise control. That way, you don't have to hold it in your hand and your finger does all the work! Designed by Cindy Cloward of Riley Blake Designs.

Powerful

If you have many seams to rip or embroidery to remove, the powerful Electric Seam Ripper by Galaxy Notions will get the job done quickly and efficiently without any hand strain. It's also a great adaptive tool as you don't have to pick out each stitch individually.

Unpicking vs. Seam Ripping

There are many ways to use a seam ripper, but here are two of our favorite ways to remove seams quickly and easily: Instead of peeling apart the seam like a banana and ripping each individual stitch as you peel, try holding your fabric straight and taut in your fingers a section at a time as you slide the seam ripper between the two pieces of fabric. Your seam ripper should slice through the threads effortlessly as it glides between the two pieces of fabric. If it's not working well, it may be that your seam ripper is a bit dull.

Have a Ball

You might be wondering, what's the little red ball for on your seam ripper? It's meant to protect your fabric as you rip, so it should be facing downward toward your fabric. If you prefer to rest your fabric on a surface as you rip, the red ball can help your seam ripper glide through stitches more easily.

As for unpicking seams, you may want to do this if you have thinner or delicate fabrics. It also makes less of a mess to unpick instead of cutting through all the threads in one go. Unpicking seams is accomplished by taking the point of your seam ripper and clipping a stitch on the outside of your seam, not in the middle, about every ½" inch or so. When you are through, you should be able to simply pull the other thread out in its entirety, releasing the stitches. There will be shorter threads left behind in the fabric, but you can brush them away or pick them out with a pair of tweezers.

You can watch how Natalie uses her seam ripper in the "Seam Ripping 101" episode of the *Final Stitch* on our YouTube channel.

It's sure to make your sewing experience much easier!

Gift Wrapping with Fabric
Patchwork Tumbler Quilt

In the wee hours of Christmas morning, carefully wrapped gifts are spread beneath the tree. It's a sight as lovely as a picture. Pretty paper. Crisp folds. Elegantly-tied bows.

One hour later, the idyllic scene has changed. The gifts have been opened, the Christmas surprises revealed. There have been squeals of delight and grateful hugs, and the floor is covered with piles of crumpled wrapping paper. This moment is charming, too, in it's own cozy way, but it sure is a shame to toss out all that pretty paper. This year, consider swapping your gift wrap for something homemade and eco-friendly.

In Japan, when gifts are given, they are often wrapped with squares of fabric called furoshiki. These beautiful cloths are made of silk, cotton, rayon, or nylon. They are hemmed, carefully wrapped around the gift, and secured with ribbon or artful knots or tucks.

It's an elegant treatment for any gift, but that's not all. Furoshiki can be used again and again in dozens of different ways. It can be folded and knotted into a reusable shopping bag. It can be a scarf. It can be a tablecloth or wall hanging. And, it adds a sweet, homemade touch to your most special gifts.

The tradition of furoshiki dates back 1,200 years, when it was used to wrap the treasures of the noble class. Eventually, furoshiki found its way into everyday use among the general population, but when plastic bags became popular after World War II, furoshiki fell out of fashion.

In recent years, a greater concern for the environment has spurred a resurgence of these eco-friendly, multi-purpose cloths. In 2006, Yuriko Koike, Minister of the Environment for Japan, encouraged the public to use furoshiki in place of plastic bags, wrapping paper, and other single-use items. She developed a campaign called "Mottainai Furoshiki", a title that translates to "use furoshiki to avoid waste." Koike explained, "The Japanese word mottainai means it's a shame for something to go to waste without having made use of its potential in full."

You can make your own furoshiki using fat quarters or yardage. Cut the fabric into a square—large or small—and hem the edges for a nice finish. That's it! You've just created custom gift wrap that can be used and reused for years to come!

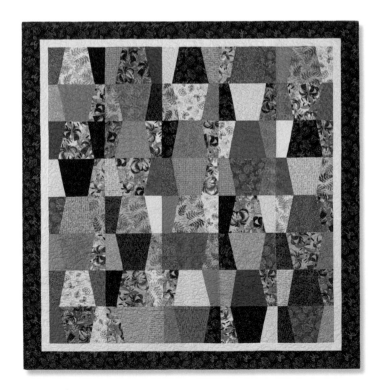

materials

QUILT SIZE
85½" x 89"

BLOCK SIZE
15" x 10" unfinished,
14½" x 9½" finished

QUILT TOP
2 packages 10" print squares

INNER BORDER
¾ yard

OUTER BORDER
1¼ yards

BINDING
¾ yard

BACKING
8¼ yards* - vertical seam(s)
    or 2¾ yards of 108" wide

OTHER
Missouri Star Large Tumbler
Template for 10" Squares

***Note**: If the width of your
backing fabric is more than
44", you may only need
5½ yards.*

SAMPLE QUILT
Carolina Lilies by Robin
    Pickens for Moda Fabrics

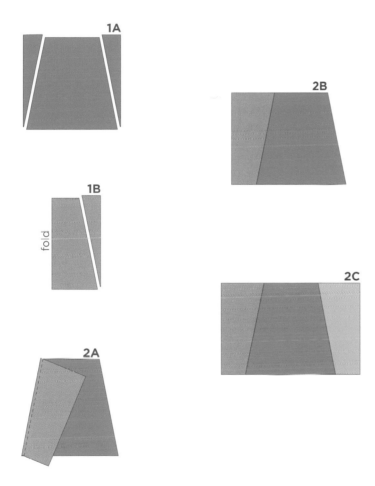

1 cut

Note: We chose to cut each square in both packages as described below for added variety. You can set 2 squares from each package aside for another project if you wish. A **total of 40** squares from each package are needed to complete the quilt.

Keep all of the squares from each package organized together.

From each square in 1 of your packages, cut a tumbler shape using the template. **1A**

From each square in the second package, fold each square in half and place the centerline of the template along the unfolded edge of the square. Cut along the slanted edge to yield half-tumbler shapes. **1B**

2 block construction

Select a full tumbler and 1 half-tumbler from each side. All 3 pieces should be of different prints. Lay the left-side tumbler atop the full tumbler, right sides facing, with the slanted edges aligned. The ends will not align but should overlap 1 another's seam line. Sew the 2 pieces together. Open and press. **2A 2B**

Repeat to sew the right-side half-tumbler to the other slanted edge of the full tumbler. **2C**

Repeat to **make 40** blocks.

Block Size: 15" x 10" unfinished, 14½" x 9½" finished

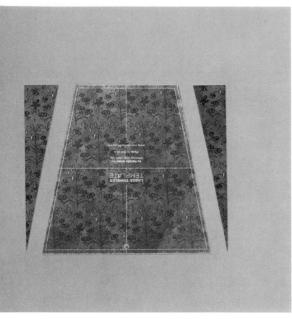

1 From each square in 1 of your packages, cut a tumbler shape using the template.

2 Fold each square in your second package in half and place the centerline of the template along the unfolded edge. Cut along the slanted edge to yield 2 half-tumbler shapes.

3 Select 1 full tumbler and 1 left-side half-tumbler that are cut from different print fabrics. Sew the left-side half-tumbler to the full tumbler as shown. Notice that the ends do not align, but should meet at the seam line.

4 Open and press.

5 Select a right-side half-tumbler and sew it to the right side of the full tumbler.

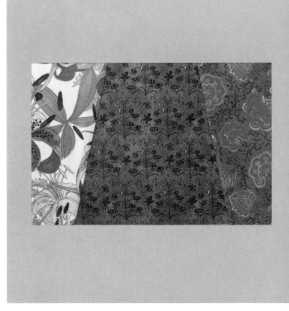

6 Open and press to complete the block.

3 arrange & sew

Refer to the diagram below to layout the blocks in **8 rows of 5**. Notice how the blocks are rotated 180° in each row. Sew the blocks together to form the rows. Press in the rows in opposite directions. Nest the seams and sew the rows together. Press.

4 inner border

From the inner border fabric, cut (8) 2½" strips across the width of the fabric. Sew the strips together to form 1 long strip. Cut the inner borders from this strip. Refer to Borders (pg. 118) in the Construction Basics to measure, cut, and attach the borders. The strip lengths are approximately 76½" for the sides and 77" for the top and bottom.

5 outer border

From the outer border fabric, cut (8) 5" strips across the width of the fabric. Sew the strips together to form 1 long strip. Cut the outer borders from this strip. Refer to Borders (pg. 118) in the Construction Basics to measure, cut, and attach the borders. The strip lengths are approximately 80½" for the sides and 86" for the top and bottom.

6 quilt & bind

Layer the quilt with batting and backing, then quilt. See Construction Basics (pg. 118) to add binding and finish your quilt.

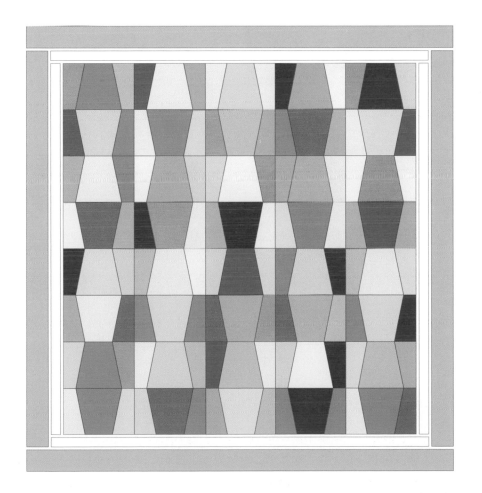

Made by Mamaw
Star Sashed Nine-Patch Quilt

By Margaret Nichols Trim, a customer story

My mamaw, Mabel Irene Nichols, from West Virginia made quilts. Being born in 1904, quilt making was a way to use up scraps and make them into a usable and functional blanket for the cold winter nights. She would put six to eight quilts on a bed to keep you warm, since the bedrooms weren't heated. Her piecing was known to be exotic and sometimes adventurous! Back then, there were few patterns as we use today, but women would use templates cut out of thin wax paper, then traced on sturdier brown paper, laid on the fabric and cut with scissors. Then, the pieces were hand sewn into blocks.

Then, she would sew them together into a quilt top. Using a pencil, she would lightly trace her quilting pattern onto the backing, making unique designs. She would get so absorbed into her art and worked long into the night. Most of her quilts went to the family as gifts—and, we loved receiving them, but so, too, did her neighbors! She taught her two daughters how to quilt so they could help her make quilts for those less fortunate than them.

Later in life, she started making "fancy" quilts, and entered those quilts into fairs where she won many ribbons. It was about this time that some of her quilts caught the eye of someone from the Appalachian Arts Association and she became a respected member. She received commissions from all parts of the country for her quilts. Her eldest daughter, Charlotte, inherited her templates and quilted in the same fashion as my mamaw.

Her second daughter, Doris, quilted in the "new" fashion, using patterns rather than templates. I, her granddaughter born from her oldest son, was lucky to inherit a few of her quilts, including one for which she won a blue ribbon. I still have a few threadbare quilts that I slept under when I was a young girl.

I've spent so much time admiring these quilts, protecting them and studying the block and quilting patterns that I felt drawn to making one. So, at the age of 63, with a $25 Singer sewing machine purchased at a garage sale, pastel cotton fabric and white cotton backing, I made my first quilt following a simple pattern. I learned I couldn't sew a straight line nor could I cut worth a hoot, but I could "sew" my mistakes into a quilt top. I keep it as a reminder that I, too, can make something beautiful out of pieces. This same feeling must be what my mamaw felt when she completed her first quilt. All my quilts, in the same manner as my mamaw, are given to family or donated to a local charity.

Even though I didn't learn to make a quilt at the knees of my mamaw or aunts, I am inspired by their works of art. Each time I quilt, I feel close to these amazing women and appreciate all the work they did to help others. I have learned that all quilters, whether they be young or old, male or female, relatives or neighbors, are the gentlest, kindest and the most selfless folks on this earth.

materials

QUILT SIZE
65" x 65"

BLOCK SIZE
16½" unfinished, 16" finished

QUILT TOP
1 roll of 2½" print strips
1 yard background fabric

SASHING & INNER BORDER
1 yard

OUTER BORDER
1 yard

BINDING
¾ yard

BACKING
4 yards - vertical seam(s)
    or 2 yards of 108" wide

SAMPLE QUILT
Persis by Studio RK
    for Robert Kaufman Fabrics

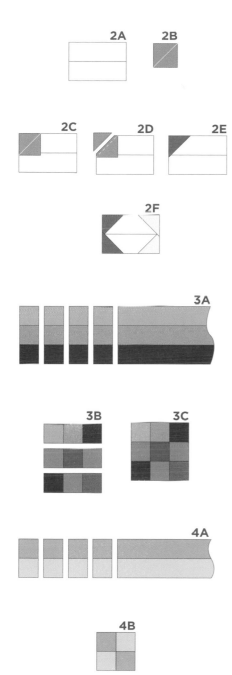

2A 2B

2C 2D 2E

2F

3A

3B 3C

4A

4B

1 sort & cut

From your roll of strips, select 9 strips—5 light and 4 dark strips—and cut (16) 2½" squares from each strip for a **total of 144**. Set the remaining strips aside for now.

Tip: You'll use 4 pairs of 2 matching strips in section 4. You might like to select and separate those out now.

From your background fabric, cut (12) 2½" strips across the width of the fabric. Subcut a **total of (72)** 2½" x 6½" rectangles.

2 sew star leg units

Pick up (2) 2½" x 6½" background rectangles. Lay them right sides together and then sew down 1 long edge. Open and press. **Make 36** units. **2A**

Pick up the 2½" print squares and mark a diagonal line on the reverse side of each square. Organize your marked print squares in 18 groups of 8 matching squares. **2B**

Select 1 group of 8 light squares and 1 group of 8 dark squares. **Note**: Light and dark for this portion of the pattern are in relationship to 1 another in each unit and not in relationship to the entire quilt. 1 set of light squares will need to be used as a set of dark squares, so be sure to pair this set with an even lighter set of squares for the most contrast possible.

Place a dark square on a corner of a unit as shown. Sew on the marked line and trim the excess ¼" away from the sewn seam. Fold the snowballed corner over the seam and press. **2C 2D 2E**

Snowball the 3 remaining corners of the unit using the squares in the groups you selected as shown. Notice that 1 short side of each unit has light snowballed corners and the other has dark. **Make 9** groups of 4 matching units. **2F**

3 sew nine-patches

Sew 3 strips together lengthwise, as shown. Press. **Make 7**. Cut the strip sets into a **total of (108)** 2½" segments. **3A**

Pick up 3 different segments and arrange them in 3 rows. Sew the rows together and press. **Make 36. 3B 3C**

4 sew four-patches

Select 2 pairs of 2 matching strips. Sew 1 strip from each matching pair together lengthwise. Press. **Make 2**. Cut the strip sets into a **total of (18)** 2½" segments. **4A**

Pick up 2 segments and place them right sides together with the seams nested and opposite fabrics touching. Sew together on 1 side, perpendicular to the sewn seam. Open and press. **Make 9. 4B**

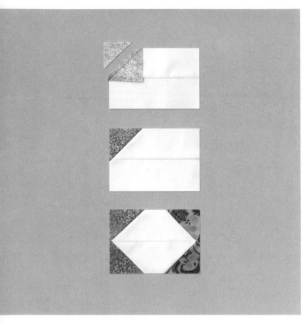

1 Sew 2 background rectangles together. Press. Place a light square with a marked diagonal line atop the background unit. Sew on the marked line, then trim the excess and press. Repeat to add a square to each corner.

2 Sew 3 different print strips together, lengthwise. Press. Cut into 2½" segments.

3 Select 3 different segments and arrange them in 3 rows as shown. Sew the rows together and press.

4 Sew 2 different strips together lengthwise. Press. Cut the strip set into 2½" segments.

5 Place 2 segments together, right sides facing with seams nested and opposite fabrics touching. Sew together along 1 long edge, crossing over the previously sewn seams. Open and press.

6 Select (4) 9-patches, 4 star leg units, and (1) 4-patch. Arrange them in 3 rows of 3 as shown. Sew together in rows and press in opposite directions. Nest the seams and sew the rows together. Press.

5 block construction

Pick up (4) 9-patches, 4 star leg units, and (1) 4-patch. Arrange the units in 3 rows of 3 as shown. Notice how the light snowballed corners of the star leg units are placed towards the center. **5A**

Sew the units together in rows. Press the seams in opposite directions. Nest the seams and sew the rows together. Press. **Make 9. 5B**

Block Size: 16½" unfinished, 16" finished

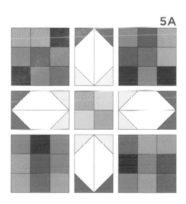

5A

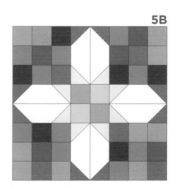

5B

6 arrange & sew

From your sashing fabric, cut (11) 2½" strips across the width of the fabric. Subcut a **total of (6)** 2½" x 16½" rectangles from 3 of the strips. Set the remaining strips aside for now.

Use the diagram below as necessary to arrange your blocks in **3 rows of 3**. Place a 2½" x 16½" rectangle in between the blocks and sew them together in rows. Press.

Sew the 2½" strips you set aside earlier together to form 1 long strip. Measure the width of your rows and cut 2 horizontal sashing strips to this length, approximately 52½". Set the remainder of the long strip aside for the inner border.

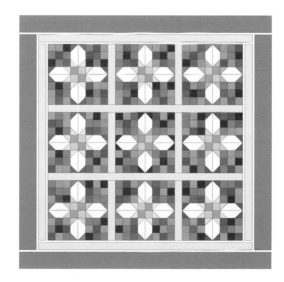

Place the horizontal sashing strips you just cut in between the rows. Sew the rows and sashing strips together to create the quilt center. Press.

7 inner border

Cut the inner borders from the long strip set aside earlier. Refer to Borders (pg. 118) in the Construction Basics to measure, cut, and attach the borders. The strip lengths are approximately 52½" for the sides and 56½" for the top and bottom.

8 outer border

From the outer border fabric, cut (6) 5" strips across the width of the fabric. Sew the strips together to form 1 long strip. Cut the outer borders from this strip. Refer to Borders (pg. 118) in the Construction Basics to measure, cut, and attach the borders. The strip lengths are approximately 56½" for the sides and 65½" for the top and bottom.

9 quilt & bind

Layer the quilt with batting and backing, then quilt. See Construction Basics (pg. 118) to add binding and finish your quilt.

Simply Charming
Tumbler Dash Quilt

In 1989, the Ladies Art Co. of St Louis, Missouri published a catalog of mail-order quilt patterns. Never before had patterns been available on such a large scale. All together, there were 400 different patterns for sale—everything from Wedding Rings to Pineapples to Bear's Paws. The prices ranged from one pattern for ten cents to fifteen patterns for a dollar.

Can you imagine the excitement of thumbing through the pages of that catalog? Hundreds of quilt patterns—some familiar, some new—just waiting to be chosen as your next patchwork project. But how could you ever pick a favorite?

Pattern #368 was a tumbler quilt pattern made with tesselating trapezoids. During the late 1800s, these quilts were often made in the style of charm quilts or beggar quilts. That is, each of the tumblers was cut from a different fabric. A quilter might dive into her own scrap bin, then turn to her friends for even more variety. Thus, an antique tumbler quilt is like a time capsule of the textiles of its era, with some quilts showcasing hundreds—or even thousands—of different 19th century fabrics.

I remember spotting a collection of the unfinished pieces of a tumbler quilt in an antique shop. The project was dated to the 1880s, with four complete hand stitched rows of tumblers.

I also saw one partial row, and dozens of loose tumblers, neatly trimmed but never sewn. There were flowers and stripes and even a diminutive dog print.

I had dozens of questions but no answers: Who started this quilt? And why didn't she finish? Did these scraps come from the shirts, dresses, and aprons of her family and friends? Did her hands ache from piecing with a needle and thread? Did she sit by the light of the fire to sew? Was this quilt to be a gift? Was it meant to grace her wintertime bed?

I'd love to know why it was abandoned. Perhaps the quilter grew bored and shifted her attention to a new pattern. (I think we're all guilty of the same!) Perhaps she was overwhelmed with day-to-day chores: Churning butter, fetching water, scrubbing laundry. Perhaps she meant to finish the quilt, but never quite found the time. I'm sure she never imagined that, 140 years later, her work-in-progress would fetch a pretty penny as a cherished historical artifact!

The tumbler quilt has remained popular for more than a century. And, thanks to modern tools and techniques, we can whip up project after project at lightning speed. Which, I suppose, is kind of a shame. Our incomplete quilts won't find their way to antique shops. They'll all be finished, cuddled, and loved for generations to come!

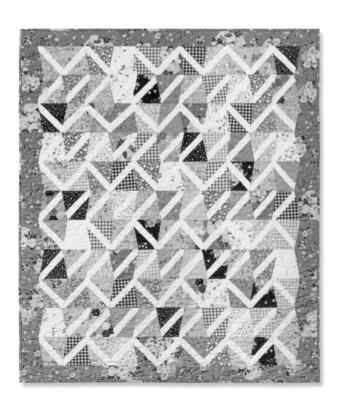

materials

QUILT SIZE
44½" x 54½"

BLOCK SIZE
5" unfinished tumbler,
4½" finished tumbler

QUILT TOP
3 packages 5" print squares
1¼ yards background fabric

BORDER
¾ yard

BINDING
½ yard

BACKING
3 yards - horizontal seam(s)

OTHER
Missouri Star Small Tumbler
Template for 5" Charm Packs

SAMPLE QUILT
Hidden Cottage by Minki Kim
for Riley Blake Designs

2A

2B

2C

2D

2E

3A

3B

3C

3D

1 cut

From the background fabric, cut (25) 1½" strips across the width of the fabric. Subcut a **total of (121)** 1½" x 7½" rectangles from the strips.

From the border fabric, cut (3) 5" strips across the width of the fabric. Use the template to subcut a **total of 22** tumblers for the side borders. Be sure to rotate the template 180° after each cut. Set the remainder of the fabric aside for the top and bottom border.

2 make units

Cut a 5" square in half diagonally. **2A**

Fold each triangle in half and carefully finger press to mark the center of the longest edge. **2B**

Fold a 1½" x 7½" background rectangle in half and finger press to mark the center. **2C**

Lay the rectangle on top of a triangle, right sides facing with creases aligned. Sew along the matched edge. Open and press. **2D**

Repeat to add the second triangle to the opposite side of the rectangle. **Make 121**. Set the remaining (5) 5" squares aside for another project. **2E**

Separate the units into 2 stacks—Stack A is made up of 36 units and Stack B is made up of 85 units.

3 cut tumblers

Select 1 unit from Stack A and rotate it so the background strip is running from the top left to the bottom right. Place the template on the unit, aligned in the lower right as shown. **3A**

Cut around the template to yield an A Tumbler. **Make 36**. **3B**

Block Size: 5" unfinished tumbler, 4½" finished tumbler

Select 1 unit from Stack B and rotate it so the background strip is running from the bottom left to the top right. Place the template on the unit, aligned in the lower left as shown. **3C**

Cut around the template to yield a B Tumbler. **Make 85**. **3D**

Block Size: 5" unfinished tumbler, 4½" finished tumbler

4 arrange & sew

Refer to the diagram on page 77 to layout the blocks in **11 rows of 11**. Pay close attention to the placement of the A and B Tumblers. Add a border tumbler to both ends of each row. Sew the blocks together to form the rows. Press in the rows in opposite directions. Nest the seams and sew the rows together. Press. **4A**

1 Cut a 5″ square in half once diagonally. Fold each triangle in half and carefully finger press to mark the center of the longest edge.

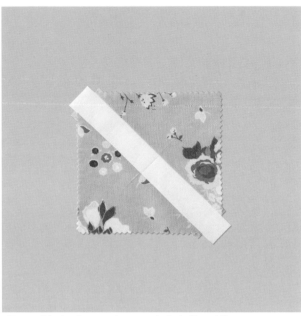

2 Fold a background rectangle in half and finger press to mark the center. Match the centers and sew the rectangle between the 2 triangles. Press. Make 121.

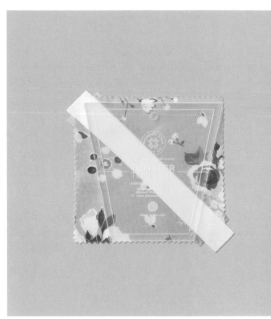

3 Rotate 1 unit as shown, then place the template on top. Align the template in the lower right corner of the unit, as shown. Cut around the template to yield an A Tumbler.

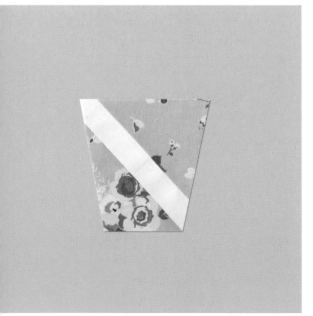

4 Repeat to make 36 A Tumblers.

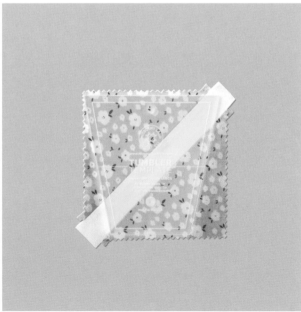

5 Rotate 1 unit as shown, then place the template on top. Align the template in the lower left corner of the unit, as shown. Cut around the template to yield a B Tumbler.

6 Repeat to make 85 B Tumblers.

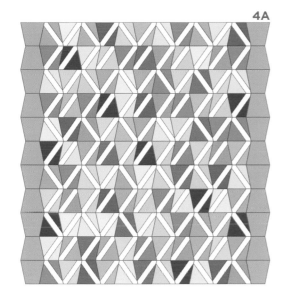

4A

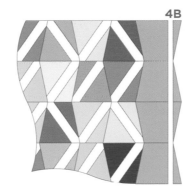

4B

Place an acrylic ruler on the sides of your quilt top, connecting the inner part of the jagged sides. Trim the jagged edges of the sides of the quilt top so it is now a rectangle that measures approximately 45" x 50". **4B**

5 border

From the border fabric, cut (3) 3" strips across the width of the fabric. Sew the strips together to form 1 long strip. Trim the borders from this strip.

Note: If your quilt top is narrower than the width of your fabric, you can trim the top and bottom border strips from (2) 3" strips and skip sewing them together.

Refer to Borders (pg. 118) in the Construction Basics to measure, cut, and attach the borders. The borders should be approximately 45" long.

6 quilt & bind

Layer the quilt with batting and backing, then quilt. See Construction Basics (pg. 118) to add binding and finish your quilt.

Talavera Tile Sew-Along
PART 6

QUILT SIZE
77" x 77"

WHOLE QUILT TOP
1 package 10" print squares
1 package of 10" Talavera Tile
squares:
- 10 fabric A squares
- 10 fabric B squares
- 7 fabric C squares
- 14 fabric D squares
- 11 fabric E squares

¼ yard fabric B
 - includes Lemon Star border
¼ yard fabric C
1½ yards fabric F
 - includes sashing and
  Lemon Star border

3¼ yards fabric G
 - includes sashing, Lemon Star
  border, and binding

BINDING
¾ yard

BACKING
4¾ yards – vertical seam(s)
 or 2½ yards 108" wide*

*Note: 2 packages of 10" print squares
can be substituted for the package
of Talavera Tile squares. You will need
a **total of (52)** 10" squares. Other
packages of squares may not have
the same number of duplicate prints
needed to match the quilt exactly.*

SASHING & FINISHING SUPPLIES
(2) 6¼" fabric G strips (cut from yardage)
(4) 3½" fabric G strips (cut from yardage)
(3) 3" fabric G strips (cut from yardage)
(2) 2⅝" fabric G strips (cut from yardage)
(13) 2½" fabric G strips (cut from yardage)

Note: *Fabric G is the only fabric used
for sashing and finishing.*

**TOTAL FABRIC REQUIRED IF YOU ARE
SELECTING YOUR OWN:**
Fabric A - 1 yard
Fabric B - 1¼ yards
Fabric C - ¾ yard
Fabric D - 1¼ yards
Fabric E - 1 yard
Fabric F - 1½ yards
Fabric G - 3¼ yards

Fabric Key

A Dark Royal
B Teal
C Sea foam
D Sunshine
E Orange
F White
G Navy

Note: Fabric G is the only fabric used for sashing and finishing. It will be helpful to stack and label the sashing pieces as you cut.

Set aside any remaining pieces not used aside for the bonus project.

1 cut

From the fabric G yardage, cut:

- (2) 6¼" strips across the width of the fabric. Subcut a **total of (8)** 6¼" x 10½" wide sashing rectangles.

- (4) 3½" strips across the width of the fabric. Subcut a **total of (8)** 3½" x 16½" Fancy Flight sashing rectangles.

- (3) 3" strips across the width of the fabric.
  - From 2 strips, subcut (7) 3" x 5½" rectangles from each strip.
  - From 1 strip, subcut (2) 3" x 5½" rectangles. Add these to those previously cut for a **total of 16** Pinwheel Party sashing rectangles.
  - Trim the remainder of the strip to 2⅝" and subcut (4) 2⅝" x 6¼" rectangles.

- (2) 2⅝" strips across the width of the fabric. Subcut (6) 2⅝" x 6¼" rectangles from each strip. Add these to the rectangles previously cut for a **total of 16** Super Easy Hourglass sashing rectangles.

- (13) 2½" strips across the width of the fabric.
  - Subcut 4 strips into a **total of (16)** 2½" x 10½" sashing rectangles.
  - Set the remaining 9 strips aside for the binding.

2A

2B

2C

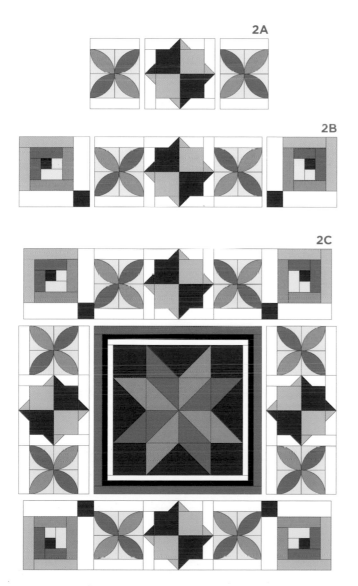

2 inner border

Select 1 sashed Orange Peel A, 1 Double Square Star, and 1 sashed Orange Peel B and arrange them in that order, as shown. Sew the sashed blocks together and press to 1 side. **Make 4** inner borders. Each inner border should measure approximately 13½" x 31½". **2A**

Sew a sashed Simple Log Cabin block to either side of an inner border. Notice that the right side Simple Log Cabin is rotated 90°. Sew the blocks to the border and press towards the sashed Simple Log Cabin blocks. **Make 2** long inner borders. Each long inner border should measure approximately 13½" x 57½". **2B**

Sew the inner borders to either side of the bordered Lemon Star block as shown. Press towards the Lemon Star block. Sew the long inner borders to the top and bottom of the quilt center. Press to 1 side. **2C**

3 outer border

Sew a 3" x 5½" fabric G rectangle to 2 opposite sides of each Pinwheel Party block. **Make 8** sashed Pinwheel Party blocks. **3A**

Sew a 2⅜" x 6¼" fabric G rectangle to the 2 fabric E sides of each Super Easy Hourglass block. **Make 8**. **3B**

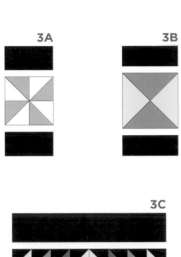

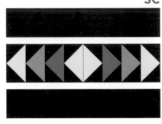

3G

Sew a 3½" x 16½" fabric G rectangle to the 2 long sides of each Fancy Flight row. **Make 4**. **3C**

Select 1 sashed Super Easy Hourglass block, 1 sashed Pinwheel Party block, (2) 2½" x 10½" fabric G sashing rectangles, and (1) 6¼" x 10½" fabric G sashing rectangle and arrange them as shown. Sew the units together to create an outer border section. **Make 8**. **3D**

Arrange an outer border section on either side of a sashed Fancy Flight row as shown. Notice that the right side outer border section is rotated 180°. Sew the sections together to create an outer border. **Make 4**. Each outer border should measure approximately 10½" x 57½". **3E**

Sew a Studio Star block to either end of an outer border to create a long outer border. Press towards the center. **Make 2**. Each long outer border should measure approximately 10½" x 77½". **3F**

Sew an outer border to either side of the quilt center. Press towards the outer border. Sew a long outer border to the top and bottom of the quilt center. Press to complete the quilt top. **3G**

4 quilt & bind

Layer the quilt with batting and backing, then quilt. After the quilting is complete, see Construction Basics (pg. 118) to add binding and finish your quilt.

Bound in Secrets and Lies

PART SIX: A TEMPLATE FOR MURDER

a fiction novella, in six parts written by **Hillary Doan Sperry**

Mena shut the door behind her and dashed down to the car. Jenny dropped the scissors and backed up. She'd only managed to clip a few of the threads but there was no way to finish now.

"What are you doing?" Mena whispered, her hand out to keep Jenny from moving. "You can't be here."

Jenny's gaze skipped between the quilts and Mena and the door where Charlie could emerge any minute.

"I'm sorry I was—I was—" How did she explain herself this time? Mena picked up the scissors and shoved them inside the layers of quilts. "It's fine. Just go, quickly."

When Jenny realized Mena wasn't going to call Charlie her brain shifted back to it's inquisitive nature. "What's going on with all this?"

"I can't tell you that. Charlie's coming. You need to go."

Jenny backed up into the bushes near the driveway and paused. "You know this is hurting people right?"

Mena's eyes teared up and she swallowed hard and shook her head. "I don't want to hurt anyone. I don't know how it got this crazy."

Jenny took a step back and Mena's eyes widened, her hands flying up to stop her. "You have to go. Just, come back tonight, after dark."

"What's happening tonight?" Jenny stood struggling with a desire to retreat and the need for information.

The door creaked on the porch. "Just be here," Mena hissed and slammed the door shut.

Charlie Reyes stepped out onto the porch, and Jenny ducked, slipping behind the large bush and around an old tool shed.

"Charlie," Mena's voice called to her husband. "I was just counting them. I'm nervous—"

Jenny reached the sidewalk and started quickly down the road, the sound of Mena's voice going silent. She pulled out her phone and dialed Officer Wilkins. He was going to be busy tonight.

It was hours later, after she'd informed the police and the sun had set, that she found herself leaning in the window of the police cruiser begging to see Mena's warning through. "What if I forgot to tell you something?" Jenny said.

The officers had parked down the street neighboring the Reyes's home. Even in the dark they had a clear view of the Reyes's car.

"Is there anything you forgot to mention?" Officer Dunn still wore his sunglasses even though it was after ten o'clock. He pulled them down to look at her and removed them as if just realizing it was night time.

"I don't know. I can't remember!" Jenny said in her most emphatic whisper.

Dunn raised an eyebrow at her, and Officer Wilkins leaned over. "Mrs. Doan, I promise we'll get the bad guy here. If Charlie is Mish, we'll find the evidence and he'll convict himself. You don't have to do it."

She let out a breath and stepped back. It seemed like nobody believed that she could be useful. Jenny nodded. "I guess I'll go home."

She couldn't go home.

She got in her car and looked at the pile of greeting cards she'd been meaning to take to Cherry. She'd go set them on Cherry's porch even if it was late.

She walked them over to the little, yellow cottage with the flower boxes that even in the moonlight looked bright and cheerful.

She'd barely stepped on the porch when the light came on and Cherry's voice rang through the little doorbell mounted there. "Jenny? What are you doing here? Hold on, I'll be right out."

"Oh, it's nothing," Jenny said, but Cherry didn't answer. The door opened, and Jenny stood there sheepishly. "I was dropping off some letters I wanted to have you address tomorrow."

"They must have been important." Cherry gave her a skeptical look and took the letters.

"No, but since you're up, I should give you the fabric samples too. They're in my car, just a second." Jenny turned, and Cherry stepped off the porch with her.

"I'll come too. It's nice to see you. I was just sitting up there watching a show." Cherry's Southern accent made Jenny feel like it would have been something set under Georgian oaks, or with women in wide brimmed hats sipping sweet tea in the Texas sunshine.

An engine revved, breaking through Jenny's imaginings, and she pulled Cherry to a stop only a few steps from her car. A truck had pulled up in front of the Reyes's drive, and two figures emerged from the house to meet Charlie.

Jenny held her finger up to keep Cherry quiet. She nodded and gave a questioning look, but Jenny shook her head as she watched Jed get out of the vehicle and the three of them drop bag after bag of something in the back of his truck.

"Of course," Jenny whispered. "They had way too many quilts on that list to transport them all themselves."

It was obvious that Cherry still didn't understand, but as they left and the police car in front of them followed silently, Jenny took the next several minutes to fill her in.

"So, Charlie is Mish?" Cherry hissed through the dark night.

"Yes. Or we think so." Jenny leaned against the car. Every fiber of her being wanted to hop in and follow the police and the quilts, but she knew she wasn't supposed to so she glued herself to the car, prepared to talk long enough that she couldn't follow if she wanted ... which she did. Jenny glanced down the road again.

"I should probably go." As she said the words, a light turned on in the Reyes's car, illuminating the forms of two people. They looked around after a quiet conversation and the engine revved.

"Is that Mena and Charlie?" Cherry asked.

Jenny couldn't take her eyes off them. "It has to be. We can't lose them." She looked over at Cherry leaning against the car. "Get in or go home." She started the engine and Cherry jumped in, pulling the car door closed behind her.

"I'm in." She buckled and gripped the door handle as Jenny watched the car turn a corner and whipped her car out, following at as safe a distance as she dared.

***

They passed town after town on deserted back roads, praying the sound of the potholes wouldn't alert the drivers ahead to their presence.

"Where are we?" Cherry asked when the Reyeses pulled off into a little dirt driveway.

"Giving them enough time to park," Jenny replied, trying to see if their headlights had turned off. She followed them into the lot and Jenny pointed to the arched entrance. The linked circles matched the emblem stamped in the bricks.

"I should have known," Jenny said. "I have several old bricks in our porch from when this brickyard was still running. It hasn't worked in decades." Jenny parked and together they crossed the lot toward a large building.

The Reyes's car appeared to be empty but after what they'd loaded into the truck Jenny wasn't sure if she should be looking for quilts or people or what.

Tiptoeing to the door, Jenny leaned against the frame of an old window, holding a hand up to ensure Cherry remained quiet. When several seconds of silence passed, Jenny pushed the door open.

The room was covered in a thick layer of red brick dust, decorated with footprints going every direction. Old pulleys hung from the ceiling and stacks of palettes and bricks littered the corners. The remaining stockpiles of the company's lifeblood were there among the broken fragments of brick. In the center of the room was a stack of quilts.

It lay there like bait.

Jenny hesitated, but Cherry walked right in, stumbling back when Jenny grabbed her. "You can't just waltz in there. Where are the Reyeses?"

Jenny carefully scanned the room, and after a thorough check, moved forward to see if they were the quilts she thought they were.

The stack looked exactly as she'd left it in the car that morning. Jenny ran a hand across the fabric and pulled at the section of white binding she'd worked to open earlier. She tugged at the threads breaking several more and slid her fingers inside. There was the pocket, and barely half an inch inside was the paper. It was thicker than she expected and she had to wrest it out of the quilt.

What she retrieved looked like two pages. The top one was a receipt. It referenced several large numbers and listed a parcel number beneath it. A twist in Jenny's gut made it clear to her that she knew exactly what she was looking at. Cherry took the page, leaving Jenny with a deed in her hand.

This one was for a large parcel of land that ran alongside the edge of town near Grace.

"What is it?" Cherry asked.

"It's a receipt for the illegal sale of land that has been seized by the town." Jenny could feel the truth of the words settle in her bones.

Cherry flipped the page over, and gasped. "I know this house. I just thought they'd moved."

"Cherry, I think you need to call the police," Jenny said, shoving the page back into the quilt's pocket.

"I'm on it." Cherry pulled out her phone, dialing in the dark. Jenny reached for the page still in Cherry's hand as the door behind them opened.

"You should put that down," came the familiar voice of the short man from City Hall. Robert Holdin had an arm around Mena's neck as he pushed her forward into the dimly lit room. "You couldn't leave it alone, could you?"

Mena pulled against his arm. "I'm sorry, Jenny. I tried to stop him. He said you'd be here, that he was waiting for you—"

"That's enough," Robert said, shaking her body from his wrestling hold on her neck. "You were following me," he accused Jenny.

Jenny closed her eyes as the pieces fell into place. "Mish," she said quietly, knowing she should have seen it sooner.

"I prefer Commissioner, but Mish works for the rabble." He dragged Mena forward, picking up one of the loose bricks on the ground.

"Don't!" Mena sputtered, "Jed and Charlie have the rest of the quilts. He's going to kill them when he's done. Don't let—"

The brick flashed against her head, and Mena slumped in Robert's arm. He released her body, and she dropped to the dirt floor. "Nobody has to die. Well, except for her." He gestured toward Mena's still figure. "And your friend, here, and well ..." He laughed and tossed the brick in his hand. "You."

"Don't be silly," Cherry said. "We're on our way out. We don't have anything to do with these quilts."

"No, I'm afraid you know too much now. When I saw you following me, well, you made me do this." Robert tossed the brick between his hands again.

Jenny took a step back, pushing Cherry behind her. "You didn't have any right to those houses."

"Now what makes you say that? I had imminent domain. You saw Grace's notice." He waved his empty hand in the air like they were magic words.

"Only imminent domain was never approved. You never even brought it up. You just convinced that poor woman at City Hall to print you the right paperwork."

Robert laughed. "And not one of those poor saps even called the office to check. It was so easy."

"Then you used that auction to buy quilts and clean the money Merkle paid you for the land." Jenny was moving farther from the door, and Robert was getting closer.

"You would think that, but according to the receipts, Charlie bought all those quilts. Charlie filed the complaints against the houses. I had to tell the owners that the town of Hamilton was seizing their property due to negligence and they'd be paid a nominal fee or go to prison. It was a pretty simple conversation really. Until Grace came along."

CONTINUED ON PAGE 102

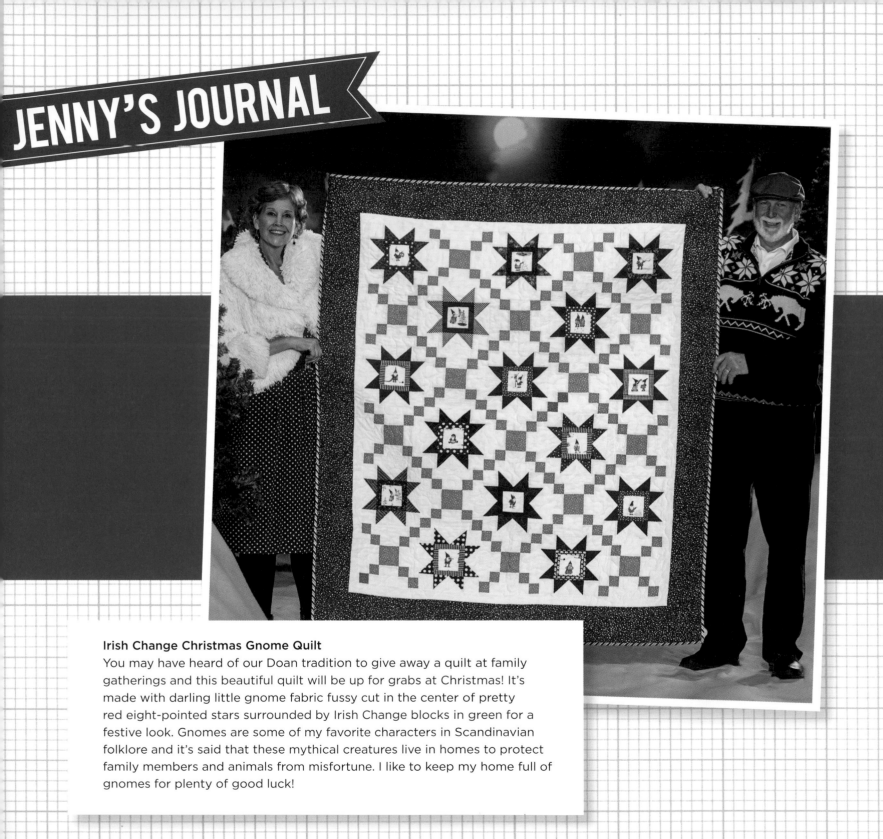

Irish Change Christmas Gnome Quilt

You may have heard of our Doan tradition to give away a quilt at family gatherings and this beautiful quilt will be up for grabs at Christmas! It's made with darling little gnome fabric fussy cut in the center of pretty red eight-pointed stars surrounded by Irish Change blocks in green for a festive look. Gnomes are some of my favorite characters in Scandinavian folklore and it's said that these mythical creatures live in homes to protect family members and animals from misfortune. I like to keep my home full of gnomes for plenty of good luck!

Winter Wonderland Quilt
by Crabapple Hill Studio

"We're happy tonight. Walking in a winter wonderland." Each day, when things calm down around our house, Ron and I like to work on embroidered quilt blocks while we watch TV in the evening. This pretty redwork quilt was a fun project for us. It features happy little snowmen frolicking in a winter wonderland surrounded by a border of some of my very favorite star quilt blocks in hues of red. It was so much fun to stitch up. You can create your very own version in any color you love. Wouldn't it be fabulous in frosty blues? Just imagine the possibilities!

Speak Your Mind
Wanderlust Quilt

One of the joys of learning other languages is finding words they've come up with that English can't fully express! It's always fascinating to think about how someone boiled down an elaborate feeling, description, or situation, added a little je ne sais quoi, and created a word that just perfectly embodies it. Some of these words, from **wanderlust** to **tchotchke**, have already been adopted by English-speakers and peppered into our day to day speech. There's so many more out there that I think should start making headways into our language!

Understanding words in other languages and learning about where they come from reminds me a lot of quilting: sewing together the smaller pieces into a brand new whole! So, let's get a word seam ripper and see where these unique euphemisms stitch together:

Waldeinsamkeit: Coming from the German words for forest (Wald) and loneliness (einsam), this word is all about the feeling of being alone in the woods; a tranquil, yet slightly spooky feeling of being surrounded only by trees (you hope!). It's a nice feeling to have for a little while, but after it gets dark it does get a little spooky!

Fernweh: From the words Fern (far, remote) and weh (hurt or sore), this word is a feeling of nostalgia or homesickness for somewhere that's really far away, or maybe even somewhere you've never been! I feel this a lot whenever I finish a good book, or watch a show set in an exotic locale.

Sobremesa: Meaning "upon the table" in Spanish, this beautiful word is all about relaxing and chatting at the table after a big meal. It's a great word for digesting while spending quality time with good friends and family!

Duende: Also coming from Spanish, this little word packs in a whole lot! It's the combination of feelings one gets when they get caught up in art, music, or dance. It's the chills you get at a beautiful piece of music, or the catching of breath at the first sight of a beautiful quilt.

Tartle: A condition that I unfortunately suffer from; forgetting someone's name right as you are about to introduce them to someone! The Scots came up with this fun sounding word for a both funny and embarrassing moment.

Of course, English doesn't have the monopoly on loanwords; many languages have borrowed words from us like jazzy and jogging, and made them their own! Another uniquely English-speaking thing that we do that other languages don't is putting exclamations in the middle of words. (Do we really do that? Abso-freakin'-lutely!)

The world is full of languages that we can learn a thing or two from. What are some of your favorite words from across the globe? Share your favorites with us on our Facebook page or email us at blockstories@missouriquiltco.com and let's spice up our language together!

materials

QUILT SIZE
70" x 79½"

BLOCK SIZE
10" unfinished, 9½" finished

QUILT TOP
1 package of 10" print squares
4½ yards of print background
  fabric* - includes inner border

OUTER BORDER
1¼ yards

BINDING
¾ yard

BACKING
5 yards - vertical seam(s)
  or 2½ yards of 108" wide

OTHER
1 package of Missouri Star
  10" Paper Piecing Squares
Water soluble fabric pen
Water soluble glue stick
  - optional
Missouri Star 10" x 10"
  Square Ruler - recommended

*__Note__: 2 rolls of 2½" background
  strips can be substituted.

SAMPLE QUILT
**English Manor Batiks and Gatsby
Batiks - Tiles Gold**
  by Kathy Engle for Island Batik

1 cut

From the print background fabric, cut (64) 2½" strips across the width of the fabric.

- Cut 24 strips into a **total of (168)** 2½" x 6" rectangles.

- Cut 21 strips into a **total of (168)** 2½" x 5" rectangles.

- Cut 12 strips into a **total of (168)** 2½" x 3" rectangles.

- Set aside 7 strips for the inner border.

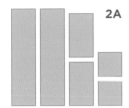

2A

2 make pieced units

From a 10" print square, cut (4) 2½" strips along the length.

- Subcut 1 strip into (2) 2½" x 4½" rectangles.

- Subcut 1 strip into (2) 2½" squares. Set the remaining 2½" x 5" rectangle aside for another project. **2A**

Select 2 each of the 2½" x 6", 2½" x 5", and 2½" x 3" background rectangles. Sew a 2½" x 3" background rectangle to the bottom of a 2½" print square

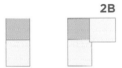

2B

2C

and press. Sew the second 2½" x 3" background rectangle to the side of the print square as shown. Press. **2B**

Lay the ruler atop the unit just made. Align the edge of the ruler from point to point and 1 raw edge of the unit with the diagonal of the ruler as shown. Trim. **Make 2** corner units. **2C**

Lay a 2½" x 6" background rectangle atop a 2½" x 4½" print rectangle, right sides facing, as shown. Mark a diagonal line on the reverse side of the background rectangle from the top left corner of the background rectangle to the bottom right corner of the print rectangle underneath. Sew along the line, then trim the excess ¼" away from the seam. Open and press. **2D**

In the same manner, sew another 2½" x 6" background rectangle to the opposite side as shown. **Make 2** short units. **2E**

Lay a 2½" x 5" background rectangle atop either end of a 2½" x 10" print rectangle. Mark, sew, trim, and press as before. **Make 2** long units. **2F**

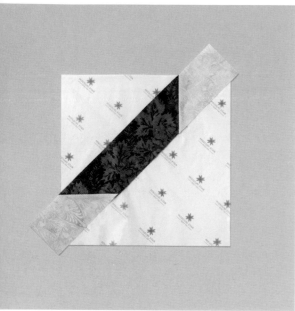

1 Lay the strip right side up, with the shorter print edge along the drawn line, and the center creases aligned. Press to adhere.

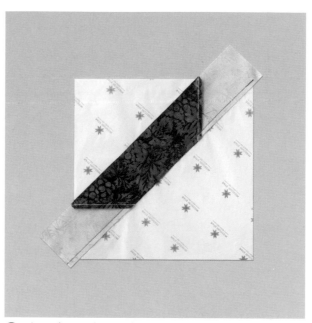

2 Lay a long unit atop the other long unit, right sides facing, center creases matched, and align the edges as shown. Pin as needed, then sew along the edge using a ¼" seam allowance.

3 Open and press. Lay a short unit atop 1 long unit, right sides facing, center creases matched, and align the edges as shown. Pin as needed, then sew along the edge.

4 Open and press. Repeat to add the other short unit to the opposite side.

5 In the same manner, lay a corner unit atop a short unit, right sides facing, center creases matched, and align the edges as shown. Sew along the edge. Repeat to the opposite side.

6 Open and press. Lay the ruler atop the sewn unit and center it along the diagonals. Trim to 10" square and remove the paper backing.

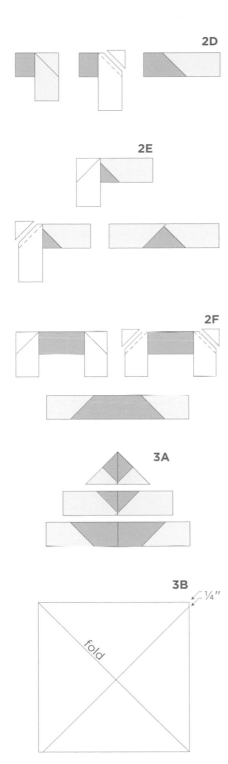

2D

2E

2F

3A

3B

¼"

fold

3 block construction

Fold each corner unit, short unit, and long unit in half and finger press a crease. **3A**

Tips: These blocks use a paper piecing method. Set your machine stitch length to 2.0 mm or shorter to prevent tearing out stitches when you remove the paper. It is helpful to have a small cutting mat, rotary cutter, small ironing mat, and iron close to your sewing machine.

Fold a foundation paper in half diagonally. Lay an acrylic ruler atop the square on the opposite angle. Align the ¼" mark of the ruler from point to point and mark a line. **3B**

Note: If you're using glue, apply a small amount to the reverse side of a long strip. If you're not using glue, you can still pin in place on the next step. Lay the strip right side up, with the shorter print edge along the line you just drew, and the center creases aligned. Press to adhere. **3C**

Lay a long unit atop the other long unit, right sides facing, center creases matched, and align the edges as shown. Pin as needed, then sew along the edge using a ¼" seam allowance. **3D**

Open and press. **3E**

Lay a short unit atop 1 long unit, right sides facing, center creases matched, and align the edges as shown. Pin as needed, then sew along the edge. **3F**

Open and press. Repeat to add the other short unit to the opposite side. **3G**

Note: As you continue to add units, you may notice that your 10″ paper underneath "shrinks." This is normal and will not affect the block.

In the same manner, lay a corner unit atop a short unit, right sides facing, center creases matched, and align the edges as shown. Sew along the edge. Repeat to the opposite side. Open and press. **3H 3I**

Lay the ruler atop the sewn unit and center it along the diagonals. Trim to 10″ square and remove the paper backing. **Make 42**. **3J**

Block Size: 10″ unfinished, 9½″ finished

3C

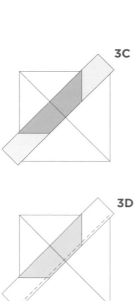

3D

3E

3F

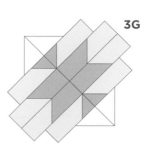

3G

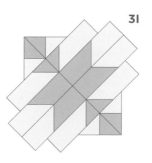

3H

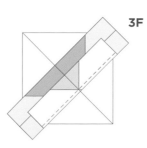

3I

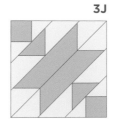

3J

4 arrange & sew

Refer to the diagram on the left to lay out your units in **7 rows of 6**. Sew the blocks together in rows. Press the seams in opposite directions. Nest the seams and sew the rows together. Press.

5 inner border

Sew the 7 background strips together to make 1 long strip. Trim the borders from this strip. Refer to Borders (pg. 118) in the Construction Basics to measure, cut, and attach the borders. The strip lengths are approximately 67" for the sides and 61½" for the top and bottom.

6 outer border

Cut (7) 5" strips across the width of the outer border fabric. Sew the strips together to make 1 long strip. Trim the borders from this strip. Refer to Borders (pg. 118) in the Construction Basics to measure, cut, and attach the borders. The lengths are approximately 71" for the sides and 70½" for the top and bottom.

7 quilt & bind

Layer the quilt with batting and backing, then quilt. After the quilting is complete, see Construction Basics (pg. 118) to add binding and finish your quilt.

All Dressed Up for the Winter
Penguin March Garland

As the weather turns cold, we can learn a lesson or two from the mighty emperor penguin. Year after year, she weathers the harshest of winters, and she does it with grace and style. But how?

First up? Quilts! Well, sort of: the emperor penguin is wrapped in four thick layers of overlapping feathers. All that downy-soft plumage keeps her toasty warm, even when bitterly cold winds blast across the antarctic coast at a deadly -40 degrees. If she were to make up a wintertime bed, I'm sure she would pile quilts up to the roof!

Next? Snacks! To prepare for winter, the penguin doubles her food intake in order to build up the thick layer of blubber under her skin. She is not worried about dimples or lumps, she knows that extra fat will keep her toasty warm, even as she dives through sub-freezing ocean temps. Winter is no time to lose sleep over calories!

Third? Good friends! On especially cold days, emperor penguins snuggle together in groups of hundreds or even thousands. They rotate from the outside to the inside, giving each penguin the chance to bask in the warmth at the center of the group.

These community snuggles are so effective, the center of the huddle can reach an elegant 75 degrees! Oh, what a difference dependable friends can make!

And, finally? A little romance, a lot of self-care, and the joys of family togetherness. After a whirlwind courtship, a female penguin lays a single egg, which is entrusted to her loyal mate for incubation. Then, she's off on a nine-week girls' trip filled with plenty of swimming and tasty food.

For sixty-five days, her gallant beau balances the egg on his feet, keeping it warm and safe with a quilt-like layer of cozy, feathered skin called a brood pouch. When the fluffy bundle of joy finally hatches, Momma returns from the sea to feed her sweet baby while Dad heads to the ocean in search of his first meal in one hundred days. For the next several weeks, they work together to care for their chick, sharing the duties of penguin parenthood as they welcome the arrival of spring at the South Pole.

This year, when the winter winds blow and the streets are covered with ice, do what the penguins do: Cozy up. Have a snack. (Have two snacks!) Support your friends. Take care of yourself. And, most important of all, treasure your dear ones and the moments you spend together. After all, spring will be here before you know it!

materials

PENGUIN SIZE
7½" x 7½"

PENGUIN SUPPLIES
(4) 10" dark print squares
(4) 10" light print squares
(4) 10" squares of fusible fleece
8 buttons, ¾" - 1" size
Rainbow Classic 9" x 12"
    Felt Square - Orange
Missouri Star Circle Magic Large
    10" Circle Template - optional
1¼ yards of ribbon

SAMPLE PROJECT
A variety of Grunge by BasicGrey
    for Moda

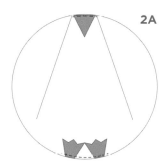

2A

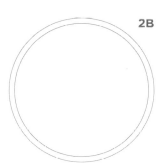

2B

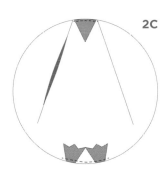

2C

2D

1 cut

Templates for this project can be found at **msqc.co/penguin-march**. Print and cut out each template. Use the circle template and cut a circle from each 10" print square.

Trace the large circle template on each fusible fleece square, then cut ¼" inside the drawn line.

Use the beak template to trace and cut 4 beaks from the orange felt.

Use the foot template to trace and cut 8 feet from the orange felt.

2 penguin construction

Choose a light print circle for the penguin's belly and place it right side up. Lay the penguin placement guide atop the circle and mark the fold lines and slit along the sides and the placement for the beak and feet.

Note: Make small marks at the edge for the beak and feet and do not mark the fold lines all the way to the bottom of the circle—the marks will not show once the penguin is sewn and folded. Arrange the beak at the top and the feet at the bottom between the marks, as shown. Baste in place ⅛" from the circle's edge. **2A**

Center the fusible fleece on the belly circle with the glue (bumpy) side of the fleece touching the reverse side of the fabric. Adhere in place following the manufacturer's directions. **2B**

Turn the fused belly circle over. Cut the slit through the fabric and fleece as marked. **2C**

Layer the fused belly circle on a dark print circle, right sides facing. Sew around the edge of the circles using a ¼" seam allowance and backstitching at the end. **2D**

Turn the circles right sides out through the slit. Push out the edges and press. **2E**

Fold the wings in along the marked fold lines and press. **2F**

Fold the top down until the beak fits between the wings, approximately 2½". Press. **2G**

Pin in place as needed. Add buttons for eyes on either side of the beak at, or just above, the corner of the fold. **Note**: Attach the buttons through the head and wing portions. You can also attach to the back section, but do not sew all the way through to the back side. Repeat to **make 4**. **2H**

Tip: String yarn through the top fold and hang your penguins.

Hang up your funny friends and enjoy them all winter long!

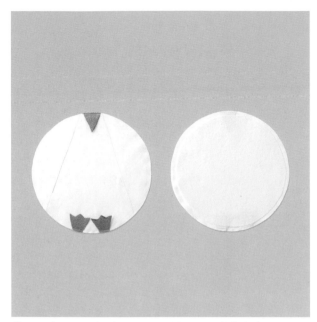

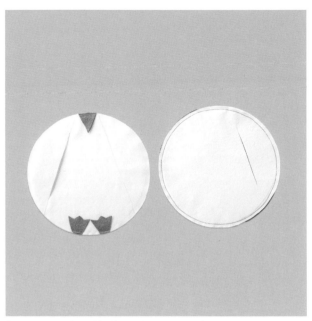

1 Lay the penguin placement guide atop a light belly circle and mark the fold lines and slit along the sides and the placement for the beak and feet. Arrange the beak and the feet between the marks, as shown. Baste in place. Center the fusible fleece on the reverse side of the belly circle and adhere.

2 Turn the fused belly circle over. Cut the slit through the fabric and fleece as marked. Layer the fused belly circle on a dark print circle, right sides facing. Sew around the edge of the circles.

3 Turn the circles right sides out through the slit. Push out the edges and press. Fold the wings in along the marked fold lines and press.

4 Fold the top down until the beak fits between the wings, approximately 2½". Press. Pin in place as needed. Add buttons for eyes on either side of the beak at, or just above, the corner of the fold.

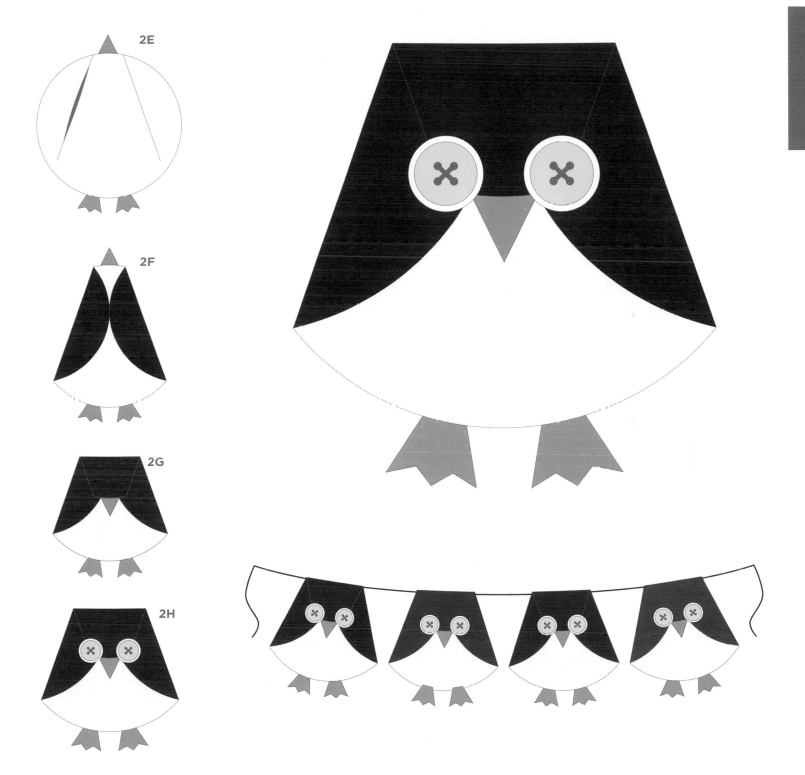

2E

2F

2G

2H

CONTINUED FROM PAGE 85

"And she wouldn't back down," Knowing the truth as Robert crossed the room toward them wasn't making Jenny feel any better.

"Grace wouldn't back down. I thought Jed would be able to make her see reason or get rid of her but that didn't work out. See, Jenny, no one was supposed to know I was involved in this. I'm an upstanding citizen. I'm on track to become mayor. Do you think they'll ever make me mayor if they know my money came from illegal avenues? No." He paused and shook his head. "I'm sorry, but you and your friend will have to go."

He stepped forward, and Cherry flailed her arms over her head. Robert jumped back, startled by the sudden movement, but he knocked Cherry to the side with his empty fist.

"Oh, come on you're making this too easy." Robert laughed.

Jenny circled around him but couldn't quite make it to Cherry. All she had within reach was the pile of quilts and deeds inside them.

He chuckled. "It doesn't matter which side of the building we're on when you die. You're still going to die."

Jenny backed up, grabbing one of the quilts and tossed it at him in a fat bundle.

He batted it away as Jenny threw another and another. Something clattered to the floor as Robert growled, his feet caught in the fabric. "Enough!"

A pair of scissors lay at her feet. The same ones she'd used and stuffed between the quilts when they were in the car. She grabbed them aiming their sharp point at him.

"What are you going to do with those?" Robert taunted, "Shorten my sleeves?"

"I can be far more dangerous than that." Jenny threatened, but it was empty and he knew it.

She threw another quilt at him, and Robert stumbled his way around it. "I'm tired of playing games, Mrs. Doan. Your time is up. Why don't you take your best shot." He laughed tossing the brick in the air.

Jenny lunged forward a half-step and Robert jerked back, alarmed that she'd come for him. Then she turned, running for the far wall.

"Get back here, Mrs. Doan!" Robert called after her.

Jenny ignored him. There, against the wall, one of the pulleys hung from a rotting rope. Jenny grabbed a brick and tossed it behind her. She could hear the commissioner jump but it hadn't stopped him. Jenny followed the line of the pulley and immediately raised her scissors cutting at the few broken fibers that were holding the rope together.

"Jenny!" Cherry called as the scissors sliced through the last of the decrepit fibers. Jenny spun around to see Robert look up as a pulley tumbled from the ceiling catching the end of a counter rope and swinging to the side. It caught him below the shoulder and Robert wailed as he went down.

Jenny launched herself at him. "Cherry! I need a quilt." Cherry scrambled to the scattered quilts and the two women wrapped the dazed man in a tight roll of quilts until he couldn't move.

"Did that just happen?" Jenny asked softly, her back against the tightly rolled criminal.

Cherry grinned. "I knew you could do it."

"I think you should call the police now."

"It's already done," Cherry said, holding up her phone. "I never hung up."

***

Jenny gripped Ron's hand as they walked up the steps to Grace's home the next day. The night before had been terrifying, but returning Grace's quilt with the stolen deed to her house had made everything feel complete.

Grace answered the door with a long hug for Jenny. "Ron, you have an amazing wife here, and I have an amazing friend." She shook her head. "I don't know how I would have made it out of this situation if you hadn't helped me. I'm still shocked that so many people listened to Charlie and gave up their properties ... I almost listened to him. I fully expected that I was going to have to move."

Cherry was inside talking to Officer Wilkins, a fully conscious Mena sitting between them.

"Oh, thank goodness you're all right." Jenny had hoped that she'd be okay.

Mena smiled weakly. "I'll be using a lot of painkillers, but I'm feeling better." She looked at Officer Wilkins. "I'll be spending a lot of time filling him in on some things too."

Wilkins nodded to her. "Mrs. Doan, I was headed to your house next. I, uh, want to thank you for your help."

Jenny nodded and bit her lip. "Is Jed here?"

Wilkins looked to Grace who suddenly appeared very busy. He gestured for Jenny to follow him onto the porch. "Jed's not here. It was he and Charlie that took the bulk of the quilts to a meeting point outside of town. We caught them handing over the deeds to the vice president of Merkle. All three of them will be facing criminal charges."

Jenny hated to think of the pain that would cause Grace, but she nodded in response. "I knew it would happen. I'm glad it's not for the wrong reasons."

Wilkins crossed his arms and looked at her. "Now you know this is not something you can keep doing, Mrs. Doan. Playing these games with the bad guys isn't something you can usually get out of with scissors and a quilt."

Jenny tried not to chuckle, and her levity dried up when his glare pinned her down. The door opened, and Ron came outside. "Can I take my wife back, Officer?"

"Can you make sure she doesn't get wrapped up in any more of my investigations?" Officer Wilkins asked.

Ron raised an eyebrow. "I can't promise any such thing. She's not one to just do what I say."

Jenny looked up at her husband and let the warmth of gratitude swell in her heart as she wrapped an arm around him. "He's right, Officer. I'm really sorry about that, but as for Commissioner Holdin," she gave him a wink and squeezed Ron, "you're welcome."

THE END

Skyward

QUILT SIZE
56½" x 56½"

BLOCK SIZE
10" unfinished, 9½" finished

QUILT TOP
1 roll of 2½" print strips
1½ yards of accent fabric
  - includes border

BINDING
½ yard

BACKING
3¾ yards - horizontal seam(s)

OTHER
Missouri Star Small Periwinkle
  (Wacky Web) Template
  for 5" Charm Packs
1 package of Missouri Star
  10" Paper Piecing Squares
Water soluble glue stick or pen

SAMPLE QUILT
Lace & Grace Batiks by Island Batik

QUILTING PATTERN
Meander

PATTERN
P. 24

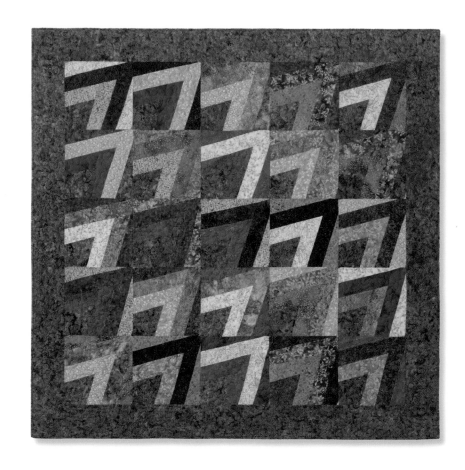

Candy Lane

QUILT SIZE
70" x 70"

BLOCK SIZE
10" unfinished, 9½" finished

QUILT TOP
1 roll of 2½" print strips
1 roll of 1½" background strips
  - includes inner border

OUTER BORDER
1¼ yards

BINDING
¾ yard

BACKING
4½ yards - vertical seam(s)
  or 2¼ yards of 108" wide

OTHER
1 package of Missouri Star
  10" Paper Piecing Squares
Water soluble glue stick or pen

SAMPLE QUILT
Kaffe Fassett Collective - August 2021
  Bright Colorway by Kaffe Fassett for
  FreeSpirit Fabrics

QUILTING PATTERN
Flowers

PATTERN
P. 30

Flower Chain

QUILT SIZE
75½" x 85"

BLOCK SIZE
10" unfinished, 9½" finished

QUILT TOP
3 packages of 5" print squares
1¼ yards of accent fabric
4½ yards of background fabric

BORDER
1¼ yards

BINDING
¾ yard

BACKING
5¼ yards - vertical seam(s)
   or 2¾ yards of 108" wide

OPTIONAL
Clearly Perfect Slotted Trimmer A
Missouri Star 10" Square Template

SAMPLE QUILT
Moonstone by Laundry Basket Quilts
   for Andover Fabric
Bella Solids - Blush by Moda Fabrics,
Kona Cotton - Silver by Robert
   Kaufman Fabrics

QUILTING PATTERN
Deb Feathers

PATTERN
P. 36

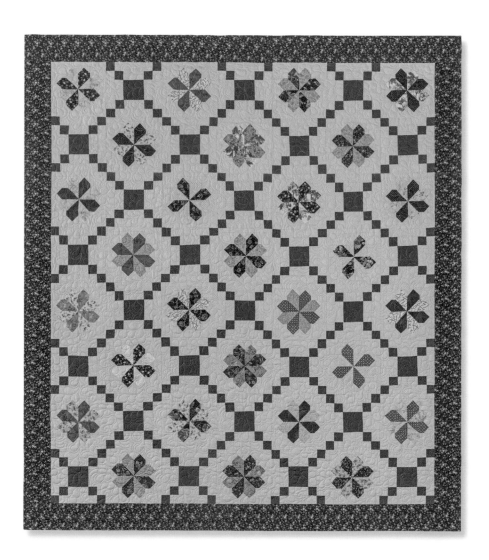

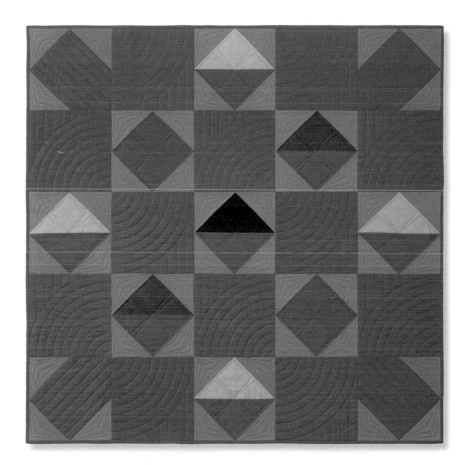

Jewel Quilt
designed by Christopher Thompson

QUILT SIZE
50" x 50"

BLOCK SIZE
10½" unfinished, 10" finished

QUILT TOP
¼ yard blue solid*
¼ yard pink solid*
¼ yard fuchsia solid*
¼ yard yellow solid*
1 yard aqua solid
2 yards teal solid

BINDING
½ yard

BACKING
3¼ yards - horizontal seam(s)

__Note__: Fat quarters may be substituted for the ¼ yard cuts.

SAMPLE QUILT
Confetti Cottons by Riley Blake
Pieced by Christopher Thompson
   (The Tattooed Quilter)

QUILTING PATTERN
Custom Quilted by Chelsea Fitzgerald
   (Cuddle Up Quilts)

PATTERN
P. 44

Four-Patch Tumbler

QUILT SIZE
43½" x 53½"

BLOCK SIZE
5" unfinished tumbler,
4½" finished tumbler

QUILT TOP
1 package of 5" print squares
¾ yard of background fabric
  - includes inner border
½ yard of accent fabric

OUTER BORDER
1 yard

BINDING
½ yard

BACKING
3 yards - horizontal seam(s)

OTHER
Missouri Star Small Tumbler
  Template for 5" Charm Packs

SAMPLE QUILT
Mary Ann's Gift 1850-1880
  by Betsy Chutchian for Moda Fabrics

QUILTING PATTERN
Simply Swirly

PATTERN
P. 50

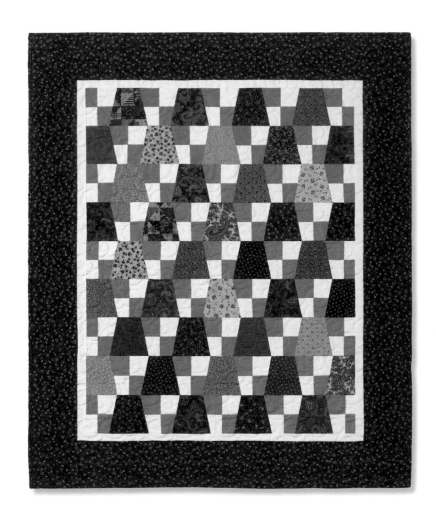

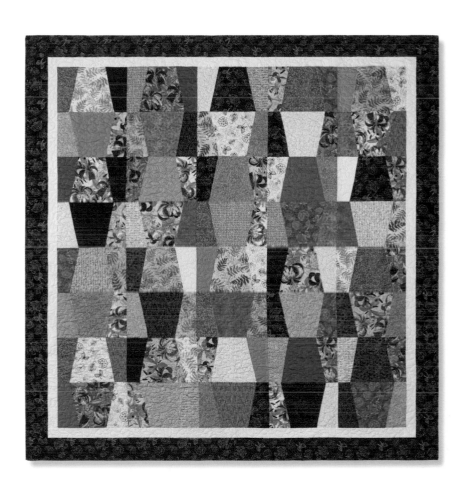

Patchwork Tumbler

QUILT SIZE
85½" x 89"

BLOCK SIZE
15" x 10" unfinished,
14½" x 9½" finished

QUILT TOP
2 packages 10" print squares

INNER BORDER
¾ yard

OUTER BORDER
1¼ yards

BINDING
¾ yard

BACKING
8¼ yards* - vertical seam(s)
or 2¾ yards of 108" wide

OTHER
Missouri Star Large Tumbler
Template for 10" Squares

*__Note__: If the width of your backing
fabric is more than 44", you may only
need 5½ yards.*

SAMPLE QUILT
Carolina Lilies by Robin Pickens
for Moda Fabrics

QUILTING PATTERN
Butterflies and Flowers

PATTERN
P. 60

Star Sashed Nine-Patch

QUILT SIZE
65" x 65"

BLOCK SIZE
16½" unfinished, 16" finished

QUILT TOP
1 roll of 2½" print strips
1 yard background fabric

SASHING & INNER BORDER
1 yard

OUTER BORDER
1 yard

BINDING
¾ yard

BACKING
4 yards - vertical seam(s)
    or 2 yards of 108" wide

SAMPLE QUILT
Persis by Studio RK
    for Robert Kaufman Fabrics

QUILTING PATTERN
Variety

PATTERN
P. 66

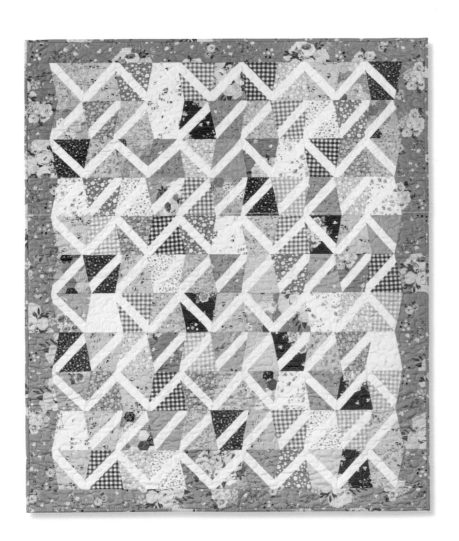

Tumbler Dash

QUILT SIZE
44½" x 54½"

BLOCK SIZE
5" unfinished tumbler,
4½" finished tumbler

QUILT TOP
3 packages 5" print squares
1¼ yards background fabric

BORDER
¾ yard

BINDING
½ yard
BACKING
3 yards - horizontal seam(s)

OTHER
Missouri Star Small Tumbler
   Template for 5" Charm Packs

SAMPLE QUILT
Hidden Cottage by Minki Kim
   for Riley Blake Designs

QUILTING PATTERN
Cotton Candy

PATTERN
P. 72

Talavera Tile Quilt

QUILT SIZE
77" x 77"

WHOLE QUILT TOP
1 package 10" print squares
1 package of 10" Talavera Tile
squares:
- 10 fabric A squares
- 10 fabric B squares
- 7 fabric C squares
- 14 fabric D squares
- 11 fabric E squares

¼ yard fabric B
  - includes Lemon Star border
¼ yard fabric C
1½ yards fabric F
  - includes sashing and
    Lemon Star border
3¼ yards fabric G
  - includes sashing,
    Lemon Star border, and binding

BINDING
¾ yard

BACKING
4¾ yards – vertical seam(s)
  or 2½ yards 108" wide *

Note: 2 packages of 10" print squares
can be substituted for the package of
Talavera Tile squares. You will need a **total
of (52)** 10" squares. Other packages of
squares may not have the same number
of duplicate prints needed to match the
quilt exactly.

PATTERN
P. 78

Wanderlust

QUILT SIZE
70" x 79½"

BLOCK SIZE
10" unfinished, 9½" finished

QUILT TOP
1 package of 10" print squares
4½ yards of print background fabric*
  - includes inner border

OUTER BORDER
1¼ yards

BINDING
¾ yard

BACKING
5 yards - vertical seam(s)
  or 2½ yards of 108" wide

OTHER
1 package of Missouri Star
  10" Paper Piecing Squares
Water soluble fabric pen
Water soluble glue stick - optional
Missouri Star 10" x 10" Square Ruler
  - recommended

*__Note__: 2 rolls of 2½" background
strips can be substituted.*

SAMPLE QUILT
**English Manor Batiks
  and Gatsby Batiks - Tiles Gold**
  by Kathy Engle for Island Batik

QUILTING PATTERN
Poppy Fields

PATTERN
P. 88

Penguin Garland

PENGUIN SIZE
7½" x 7½"

PENGUIN SUPPLIES
(4) 10" dark print squares
(4) 10" light print squares
(4) 10" squares of fusible fleece
8 buttons, ¾" - 1" size
Rainbow Classic 9" x 12"
   Felt Square - Orange
Missouri Star Circle Magic Large
   10" Circle Template - optional
1 yard of ribbon

SAMPLE PROJECT
A variety of Grunge by BasicGrey
   for Moda

PATTERN
P. 96

*Templates for project can be
   found at **msqc.co/penguin-march***

Construction Basics

General Quilting

- All seams are ¼" inch unless directions specify differently.
- Cutting instructions are given at the point when cutting is required.
- Precuts are not prewashed, therefore do not prewash other fabrics in the project.
- All strips are cut width of fabric.
- Remove all selvages.

Press Seams

- Use a steam iron on the cotton setting.
- Press the seam just as it was sewn right sides together. This "sets" the seam.
- With dark fabric on top, lift the dark fabric and press back.
- The seam allowance is pressed toward the dark side. Some patterns may direct otherwise for certain situations.
- Follow pressing arrows in the diagrams when indicated.
- Press toward borders. Pieced borders may need otherwise.
- Press diagonal seams open on binding to reduce bulk.

Borders

- Always measure the quilt top 3x before cutting borders.
- Start measuring about 4" in from each side and through the center vertically.
- Take the average of those 3 measurements.
- Cut 2 border strips to that size. Piece strips together if needed.
- Attach 1 to either side of the quilt.

- Position the border fabric on top as you sew. The feed dogs can act like rufflers. Having the border on top will prevent waviness and keep the quilt straight.
- Repeat this process for the top and bottom borders, measuring the width 3 times.
- Include the newly attached side borders in your measurements.
- Press toward the borders.

Binding

find a video tutorial at: www.msqc.co/006

- Use 2½" strips for binding.
- Sew strips end-to-end into 1 long strip with diagonal seams, aka the plus sign method (next). Press the seams open.
- Fold in half lengthwise, wrong sides together, and press.
- The entire length should equal the outside dimension of the quilt plus 15" - 20."

Plus Sign Method

find a video tutorial at: www.msqc.co/001

- Lay 1 strip across the other as if to make a plus sign, right sides together.
- Sew from top inside to bottom outside corners crossing the intersections of fabric as you sew.
- Trim excess to ¼" seam allowance.
- Press seam open.

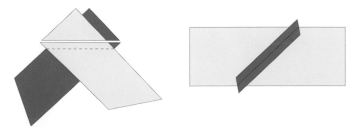

Attach Binding

- Match raw edges of folded binding to the quilt top edge.
- Leave a 10" tail at the beginning.
- Use a ¼" seam allowance.
- Start in the middle of a long straight side.

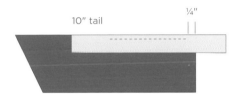

10" tail   ¼"

Miter Corners

- Stop sewing ¼" before the corner.
- Move the quilt out from under the presser foot.
- Clip the threads.
- Flip the binding up at a 90° angle to the edge just sewn.
- Fold the binding down along the next side to be sewn, aligning raw edges.
- The fold will lie along the edge just completed.
- Begin sewing on the fold.

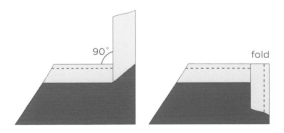

90°   fold

Close Binding

MSQC recommends The Binding Tool from TQM Products to finish binding perfectly every time.

- Stop sewing when you have 12" left to reach the start.
- Where the binding tails come together, trim the excess leaving only 2½" of overlap.
- It helps to pin or clip the quilt together at the 2 points where the binding starts and stops. This takes the pressure off of the binding tails while you work.
- Use the plus sign method to sew the 2 binding ends together, except this time when making the plus sign, match the edges. Using a pencil, mark your sewing line because you won't be able to see where the corners intersect. Sew across.

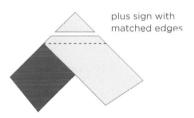

plus sign with matched edges

- Trim off the excess; press the seam open.
- Fold in half wrong sides together, and align all raw edges to the quilt top.
- Sew this last binding section to the quilt. Press.
- Turn the folded edge of the binding around to the back of the quilt and tack into place with an invisible stitch or machine stitch if you wish.